# CORE BUSINESS PROGRAM

# BUSINESS STATISTICS

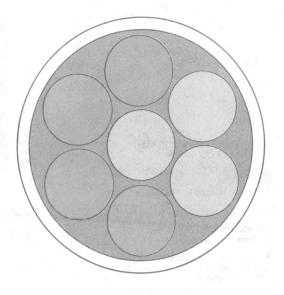

By
E.T. Martin
and
J.R. Firth

Edited by
Wilfried R. Vanhonacker

**Facts On File Publications**
460 Park Avenue South
New York, N.Y. 10016

CORE BUSINESS PROGRAM
BUSINESS STATISTICS

E.T. Martin, O.St.J., MSc, DMS, MBIM
J.R. Firth, M.A.
Edited by: Wilfried R. Vanhonacker, Ph.D.

**Copyright © 1983 by Mike Morris Productions Inc.**

Published by Facts On File, Inc.
460 Park Avenue South, New York, N.Y. 10016

First edition published in the United Kingdom in 1983 by
Mitchell Beazley London Ltd., Mill House,
87-89 Shaftesbury Avenue, London W1V 7AD, England.

**Library of Congress Cataloging in Publication Data**
Main entry under title:

  Statistics.
  (Core business program)
  Includes index.
  1. Commercial statistics–Dictionaries. 2. Statistics–Dictionaries.
I. Vanhonacker, Wilfried R. II. Title. III. Series.
HF1017.S68  1984  650'.072  83-1731
ISBN 0-87196-805-3

Printed and Bound in Great Britain
10 9 8 7 6 5 4 3 2 1

# Contents

# Introduction

The contents of this book have been deliberately designed with the business student and professional in mind, and an attempt has been made to present statistical methods and concepts in a **business** context rather than in a pure **mathematical** framework.

It is a fact that many students and practicing managers have difficulty coping with the analytic aspects of their courses or jobs, partly because of the isolated and divorced manner in which statistical methods are often taught and presented, and partly because they feel incompetent to handle the most basic numerical problems. There tends to be an aura of mystique surrounding numbers and their manipulation. Unfamiliar signs, equations, tables and graphs all look very impressive but frequently cause panic and confusion to the non-mathematician.

There is an ever-increasing demand for managers with analytic ability as well as literary skills, not only so that they can present numerical data and information which requires analysis and interpretation but, more importantly, so that they can quickly scan and understand analyses produced both from within the firm and by outside organizations. In the competitive and dynamic business world, those enterprises which are most likely to succeed, and indeed survive, are those which are capable of maximizing the use of the tools of management, including statistical analysis.

Essentially, statistics is concerned with abstracting data, classifying it and then comparing it with data obtained from similar sources so that plans and control mechanisms can be implemented. Control is the *raison d'être* of statistical analysis; it is also, as Drucker says, "the Siamese twin of planning", which in turn is a prerequisite for achieving corporate objectives. The control procedures must permeate every functional area of the firm as well as the total system of the organization. Important areas include the optimum allocation of resources – labor, machines, money and raw materials – the evaluation of machine performance, quality control requirements, stock control measures, the analysis of market research information, sales forecasting and budget preparation, and financial investment decisions. The analysis of any or all of these may provide the basis for future action.

The aim of this book is not only to remind readers of basic statistical methods but also to demonstrate their practical applications. Of course, the test is not exhaustive, and the reader is urged to consult the recommended Further Reading section, which contains several texts giving a more discursive and detailed account of statistical techniques.

I am grateful to my students and colleagues without whose stimulation and encouragement this book never would have been written, and to Mike Morris, whose good spirit and helpfulness made it all possible.

Thanks are also in order for the Literary Executor of the late Sir Ronald A. Fisher, F.R.S., to Dr. Frank Yates, F.R.S., and to Longman Group Ltd., London, for permission to reprint Tables III, IV, V from their book *Statistical Tables for Biological Agricultural and Medical Research* (6th Edition, 1974).

# Chapter 1

# Data

## COLLECTION AND REPRESENTATION

Numerical data are the raw material of statistical investigation, but the input of relevant and appropriate data is not an intermittent or periodic event; it is occurring all the time and the data are readily available from such sources as the media and government publications. Data are usually also available from other sources and are classified as **primary** or **secondary** data, depending on the method of collection and the source. **Primary data** are original data gathered specifically for the current investigation and initiated by the collecting organization. **Secondary data** are those data already gathered and perhaps published by another organization. Secondary data are invariably cheaper to obtain than primary data and, as well as being obtainable from government bodies such as the Census Bureau or the Federal Reserve, they may be acquired from trade organizations, the Conference Board, professional journals and magazines, and from public libraries, network television and private research companies (e.g., MRCA, NPD, etc.).

Too many organizations, particularly their marketing departments, decide to collect primary data without determining whether or not answers can be found from data which are already published and available. In other words, there is much merit in conducting **desk research** before stepping out to collect primary data. Millard (1972) states that

> ... desk research provides the means for the rapid assembly of relevant published material which will be of help when assessing the scope and nature of further research ... desk research can comment on the thoroughness and accuracy of the published information and provide a useful list of references and sources ... it can also highlight areas where further research is needed.

## COLLECTION OF PRIMARY DATA

### Surveys

A survey consists of the collection of data by interviewing a number of people or examining a number of objects. The subject may be the popularity of a political party or the diameter or weight of ball bearings from a flow process production line. In fact, for reasons of expense and time, a **sample** (i.e., a fraction) of the total population is taken. However, a measurement based upon a sample can only provide an *estimate*, which may be more or less close to the true population value being studied. In sampling theory, the greater the size of the sample, the more accurate the estimate will be, particularly when the population is quite heterogeneous. In addition, the sample should be selected in such a way that *every member of the population has an equal and known chance* of being selected – known as **random**

**sampling**. However, considerations of cost and practicability affect the type of sampling techniques which can be used. Modifications to random sampling have produced easier methods, although, to some extent, they affect the final accuracy. The main modifications include clustering and weighting.

### Clustering
This is a process in which interviews are not spread throughout the population but are concentrated in groups, e.g., in a restricted area such as a constituency. The reduction in accuracy depends on the size and number of clusters used and the homogeneity of the members of each cluster.

### Weighting
Sometimes differential weights need to be applied in order to yield *unbiased* estimates, e.g., the number of interviews in some specialist group may need to be increased without *at the same time* increasing the number of interviews with other groups of the population which are adequately represented. This weighting is an artificial way of increasing the representation of the population of interest in the sample.

### Bias in sampling
Bias or misrepresentation is an important potential source of error and the first source of bias may be inherent in the **sampling frame**, i.e., the list from which the sample is selected. The list may be incomplete or inaccurate so that some members of the population do not have an equal chance of being selected, e.g., telephone directories – they only contain the listed phone numbers – may not contain the names of all those who are entitled to vote. In addition, bias may also be introduced through non-response.

No survey will ever achieve 100% response, but a large element of nonresponse could invalidate the final results particularly when nonrespondents are different from respondents with respect to the information solicited.

There are four main methods of collecting information

**1.** Personal interviews.

**2.** Mail surveys.

**3.** Telephone surveys.

**1. Personal interviews** allow an experienced interviewer to modify the questions according to the responses which he receives and therefore more in-depth information may be obtained. However, if the interviewer strays too far from the carefully balanced questions, then elements of bias from either respondent or interviewer may occur. It must be stressed that market research interviewers should be selected carefully and trained thoroughly to collect information in a systematic and controlled way. In addition, this method of collecting information is usually expensive and time-consuming. However, it provides an opportunity to work with visual aids (e.g., pictures, objects, etc.) in soliciting responses to questions.

**2. Mail surveys**, while being fairly slow to reveal results, are usually the cheapest method of investigation. There are other advantages, particularly in that the survey is identically repeatable, and also that it may be the only way of contacting relevant members of the population. Unfortunately, the response rate is usually low, which may invalidate the subsequent analysis and interpretation. However, providing the questionnaire is framed correctly, interviewer bias may be discounted. In general, a mail survey will have a higher chance of success where some relationship between interviewer and respondent already exists, e.g., membership of a book club or a previous interview. Furthermore, a small reward (e.g., 50c for coffee while filling out the questionnaire) or making the survey results available to respondents might secure cooperation and increase the response rate.

**3. Telephone surveys** rule out the possibility of a random sample of the population since not everyone has a telephone. A second disadvantage is that no market research aids, such as pictures, prompt cards or advertisements, can be used. Also, it is difficult to establish any rapport and, indeed, some respondents may be positively hostile and refuse to respond to an unknown voice. Even so, the method is fast, easy to administer and relatively inexpensive. Telephone surveys are becoming increasingly useful in *industrial* market research.

## QUESTIONNAIRE DESIGN

In a market research survey, this aspect is probably the most critical phase of the whole survey. A questionnaire is simply a tool for the collection of data from potential informants and may be used in both personal interview surveys and in mail surveys. The following points are particularly relevant in the design of questionnaires.

**1.** The informant's **cooperation** must be obtained and retained.

**2.** The researcher must **communicate easily**, i.e., no ambiguities or unfamiliar words should be used. For example, in one particular survey only one-fifth of the sample understood the meaning of the word "chronology". There must be no differences in the concept or interpretation of common words such as "good" or "nice".

**3.** The respondent must be allowed to work out his own response, preferably with precoded answers and using prompt cards if necessary. It is usually difficult to analyze open-ended questions, i.e., unstructured questions requiring answers in which the informant is allowed to express opinions or value judgments.

Ideally, the questions should be capable of being answered quickly and easily using some of the following techniques.

## 1. Semantic scales

| Very good | Good | Satisfactory | Poor | Very poor |
|-----------|------|--------------|------|-----------|

## 2. Monopolar

Sweet → Not sweet

## 3. Bipolar

Sweet ↔ Sour
tendency to

## 4. The use of Skip instructions

These save time and are particularly useful in personal interviews.

| Question | Answer | Code | Skip to question |
|----------|--------|------|------------------|
| 1. Have you ever had a meal at a Chinese restaurant? | Yes<br>No | 1<br>2 | 2<br>30 |
| 2. When did you last eat in a Chinese restaurant? | One week ago<br>One month ago<br>Over six<br>  months ago | 1<br>2<br><br>3 | 3<br>25<br><br>28 |
| 3. How often do you use a Chinese restaurant? | Weekly<br>Monthly<br>Rarely | 1<br>2<br>3 | 4<br>34<br>10 |

Obviously, the questions "skipped to" must relate to the objectives of the survey and be relevant. In the above example, Question 30 might ask the following.

| 30. Why have you never had a meal at a Chinese restaurant? | Don't like the food<br>Can't afford it<br>Not near one | 1<br>2<br>3 | 35<br>38<br>40 |
|----------|--------|------|------------------|

It is always sound practice to pretest the questionnaire before using it on the sample population. The answer boxes may be precoded with numerical values to facilitate subsequent analysis.

### Classification variables
Samples may be drawn from combinations of the following types of categories.

**Area**: population, type, socio-economic groups, etc.
**Accommodation**: age, type, number of rooms, garage, rented.
**Household**: size, structure, income, car owners, mono/color TV.

**Age**: e.g., 15, 16–25, 26–35, 36–45, etc.
**Marital status**: single, married, divorced, widowed.
**Education**: high school graduate, college graduate, etc.

Whatever classification is used it must be pertinent to the research in hand and the survey must be given a title, e.g., Market Research Survey of, say, the New York Metropolitan area; over 30 years old; income above $40K; college graduate.

This classification essentially defines the population of the survey and should be consistent with the population of interest.

In all sampling, a **variate** for sampling must be selected for inspection. As sampling proceeds, a distribution of variate values is generated. This is known as a **sampling distribution**. Sampling distributions on classification variables such as age, income, marital status, etc., allow the researcher to check whether or not his sample is representative for the population he is interested in. For example. a sample of the U.S. population can be checked against census statistics to ensure representation.

To reiterate, the task of the statistician is to:

**1. measure** accurately;
**2.** couch problems in **quantitative** terms;
**3.** prepare the ground for logical **inference**.

His fact-finding, however, does not supersede judgment; rather it is complementary. Having obtained all the relevant information from samples of the population, what can be said or *inferred* about the population properties (see Figure 1)? And, having drawn inferences, what decisions can be taken? At this point the manager and statistician may part company!

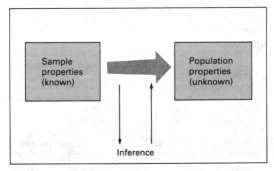

*Figure 1. Inferential analysis*

Finally, the concept of **omnibus surveys** must be mentioned. A survey among 3000 men asking one question only will cost almost as much, in terms of fieldwork costs, as a

survey of similar design and sample size but asking 20
questions. Most of the cost is incurred in traveling time and
making contact with the respondents. Omnibus surveys,
instead of being devoted to one research project, consist of a
number of subquestionnaires, each one being a survey in its
own right. The costs of the interviewer can therefore be
shared between several surveys. This technique is undertaken
almost entirely by market research specialists who offer space
on their master questionnaire.

A diagrammatic representation of a statistical study is shown
in Figure 2.

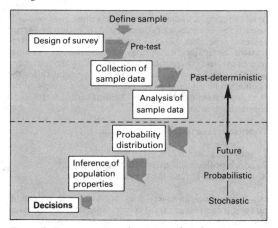

*Figure 2. Representation of a statistical study*

## DATA PRESENTATION

**Raw data** are data that are recorded in the same way or
order in which they are obtained, or in some other arbitrary
fashion. These raw and disorderly data must then be
processed and reduced into some kind of order. They must be
organized into an easily understood format, preferably by
using some form of pictorial representation such as tables,
graphs, bar charts or histograms, in order that trends or
patterns can be detected more easily. To do this, it is
necessary to **classify** the data into their peculiar *characteristics* such as width, age, height, weight, etc. There are two
basic classes of characteristics, namely measurable attributes
(or **variables**) and non-measurable attributes. A variable is
a feature characteristic of any member of a group which is
capable of being measured. One could argue that everything
is measurable in a way. The distinction is, however, that some
variables are measured with metric properties where others
are measured with nonmetric properties. For a discussion on
these issues, the reader is referred to the *Marketing Research*
book in this series. A further distinction can be made between
a **discrete** or **continuous** variable depending on the
numerical values it can take on.

**Example**
Table 1 gives the raw data of daily production figures for a
light engineering company.

| Week | Day 1 | Day 2 | Day 3 | Day 4 | Day 5 | Day 6 |
|------|-------|-------|-------|-------|-------|-------|
| 1 | 69 | 70 | 73 | 70 | 71 | 71 |
| 2 | 67 | 72 | 71 | 71 | 68 | 73 |
| 3 | 67 | 70 | 74 | 68 | 70 | 70 |
| 4 | 66 | 68 | 67 | 70 | 69 | 69 |
| 5 | 68 | 70 | 72 | 73 | 72 | 71 |
| 6 | 70 | 69 | 69 | 72 | 70 | 73 |
| 7 | 66 | 70 | 72 | 73 | 74 | 68 |
| 8 | 70 | 70 | 73 | 68 | 66 | 67 |
| 9 | 71 | 65 | 68 | 70 | 72 | 70 |
| 10 | 70 | 70 | 68 | 74 | 72 | 71 |

*Table 1. Daily production figures for a light engineering
company*

The variable is the number of units produced each day; it is
also a discrete variable because part-made units do not count.
The raw data do not convey much information, but Table 2
shows the data ordered and arranged in an **array** of
ascending orders of magnitude.

| | | | | | |
|----|----|----|----|----|----|
| 65 | 68 | 69 | 70 | 71 | 72 |
| 66 | 68 | 70 | 70 | 71 | 73 |
| 66 | 68 | 70 | 70 | 71 | 73 |
| 66 | 68 | 70 | 70 | 71 | 73 |
| 67 | 68 | 70 | 70 | 72 | 73 |
| 67 | 68 | 70 | 70 | 72 | 73 |
| 67 | 69 | 70 | 70 | 72 | 73 |
| 67 | 69 | 70 | 71 | 72 | 74 |
| 68 | 69 | 70 | 71 | 72 | 74 |
| 68 | 69 | 70 | 71 | 72 | 74 |

*Table 2. Ascending order of magnitude*

Further refinements might produce the following rearrange-
ment.

| Cell boundaries | Cell mid-point | Tabulation | Frequency |
|-----------------|----------------|------------|-----------|
| ≤ 65 | | \| | 1 |
| 66–68 | 67 | ⊪⊪⊪⊪ ⊪⊪⊪⊪ ⊪⊪⊪⊪ | 15 |
| 69–71 | 70 | ⊪⊪⊪⊪ ⊪⊪⊪⊪ ⊪⊪⊪⊪ ⊪⊪⊪⊪ ⊪⊪⊪⊪ ⊪⊪⊪⊪ ‖‖‖ | 28 |
| 72–74 | 73 | ⊪⊪⊪⊪ ⊪⊪⊪⊪ ⊪⊪⊪⊪ \| | 16 |

*Table 3. A grouped frequency distribution*

Table 2 illustrates the **range**, which is simply the difference
between the highest and lowest values, i.e., $74 - 65 = 9$.
Although Table 3 demonstrates a grouped frequency distri-

bution, in practice *it is unusual to have less than five class intervals*. A **frequency distribution** may be numerical or categorical. The distribution is said to be **numerical** if the data are grouped according to numerical size, as in Table 3. A distribution is said to be **categorical** if the data are sorted into categories according to some *qualitative* description rather than numerical size. Frequency distributions may also be represented graphically, as in Figure 3.

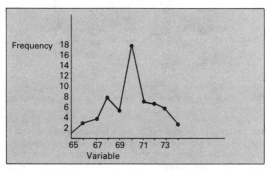

*Figure 3. A frequency distribution*

A **frequency polygon** is constructed by plotting the class frequencies of the various classes at the class (or cell) mid-points and then connecting these mid-points. Construction of a curve to show a *cumulative* distribution would result in an **ogive**. The pie chart, histogram and column chart are other forms of graphical or pictorial representation.

**The pie chart** The relative frequency of the distribution is determined and this information represented as bisectors of a circle proportional in arc length (or area or sector angle) to their value. The pie chart gives a faithful representation as a proportion of observations, but it may also give a misleading impression, for example, if a particular segment is em-phasized in some way, say, by projecting it or coloring it differently.

**The histogram** This is readily constructed from ordered data. If the number of variable values is extensive (greater than 25) then the ordinary frequency curve will reflect local variations which may not be representative of the overall picture and may lead to distortion of that overall picture. This can be overcome by grouping the data (as in Table 3). However, when the values are grouped in this way, there will be a certain amount of inherent inaccuracy. When there are too few groups, the inaccuracies become intolerable, e.g., in the extreme case, all data are placed in one group and thus knowledge of the way in which different output levels (the production figures) are achieved is lost. A histogram is simply a frequency diagram which is used to represent *grouped* data.

It consists of a number of rectangles, one corresponding to each cell, the **areas** of which represent the frequencies within the respective cells.

A segment of the variable value axis corresponds to each cell, defined by the data grouping. The vertical sides of the rectangles correspond to the cell end-points: the mid-points of the bases of the rectangles correspond to the cell mid-points. If the cell widths are all equal then the histogram resembles a **bar chart**, but if the cell widths vary, this similarity disappears. However, it should be noted that a histogram cannot be used for distributions with open classes or cells and, furthermore, if the distribution has unequal class intervals, the histogram can be very misleading. It should be remembered that it is the *area* of each rectangle which represents the frequency and *not* the height of the rectangle, i.e., if the class interval is twice as wide as the others, the height is divided by two. Figure 4 shows a typical histogram.

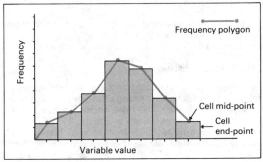

*Figure 4. A histogram*

**Column charts** are used for the aggregates of observations or aggregated observations of similar factors, as shown in Figure 5. The following data are represented by the component bar chart.

|      | Minors | Male adults | Female adults | Total |
|------|--------|-------------|---------------|-------|
| 1980 | 100    | 150         | 200           | 450   |
| 1981 | 250    | 150         | 300           | 700   |

Finally, it must be remembered that the **cumulative frequency** is the sum of all the frequencies to date.

**Relative frequency** is the frequency in a cell (or class) divided by the number of total observations.

Other pictorial representations of data include the pictogram and statistical maps or cartograms.

*Mean daily attendances at the movies*

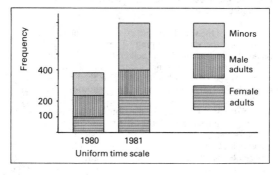

*Figure 5. A column chart (component bar chart)*

**Pictograms** use picture symbols to represent values. They do, however, lack precision.

**Statistical maps or cartograms** are used as a means of conveying information about geographical distributions, e.g., population densities, mean income, number of depots, inches of rainfall. Different values are usually indicated by different shades or colors.

Two other types of statistical data may be represented by simple diagrams. These are **categorical data**, which relate to categories or classes, and **time series data**, which are given in a time sequence such as the number of business studies degrees awarded in each of the years between 1960 and 1980. Categorical data are often represented by pie charts or bar charts as well as by tabulation, from which the length of bar charts or the sector angles of pie charts can be calculated.

**Example** The following is a distribution of selected, listed retail outlets from the Yellow Pages of the local telephone directory.

|  | Number | Bar chart length | Pie chart sector angle |
|---|---|---|---|
| Antique dealers | 75 | 2.52 in. | 37° |
| Art galleries | 132 | 4.60 in. | 65° |
| Physicians | 196 | 6.81 in. | 97° |
| Do-it-yourself stores | 155 | 5.38 in. | 76° |
| Appliance stores | 44 | 1.52 in. | 22° |
| Fish stores | 28 | 0.97 in. | 14° |
| Garden centers | 64 | 2.24 in. | 32° |
| Hi-fi equipment stores | 36 | 1.24 in. | 17° |
|  | 730 | 25.28 in. | 360° |

*Table 4. Categorical distribution*

**Time series** are usually represented by graphs, with the time measured from left to right on the *x*-axis and the other variable along the *y*-axis. Bar charts are occasionally used, especially for comparative purposes when dealing with, say, meteorological data.

# Chapter 2

# Averages

Although a high degree of data compression is obtained by using the techniques of tabulation mentioned in the previous chapter, it is more helpful in many cases to present the information in an abbreviated numerical form, particularly for purposes of comparison. A statistical set or group of data can be concisely described by reference to three types of measurement.

**1.** Measures of location, i.e., measures of central tendency or, more commonly, averages.
**2.** Measures of spread or dispersion.
**3.** Skewness, which is a measure of the tendency of the group towards symmetry or lopsidedness.

This chapter is concerned with the first measure only, namely **averages**. However, statisticians do not use the term 'averages' because it is too imprecise and has too many connotations. Nonetheless, even in its general form, the aim of an average is to describe the group which it represents and to provide a basis for comparison. There are four kinds of averages which are of particular interest.

**1.** Arithmetic mean.
**2.** Geometric mean.
**3.** Median.
**4.** Mode.

## THE ARITHMETIC MEAN

The arithmetic mean is found by adding the sum of the variables within a group and dividing the sum by the number of variables (observations) within that group. In some circumstances, the values contained in the group do not have the same degree of importance and it is therefore necessary to classify the arithmetic mean into either the *simple* mean or the *weighted* mean. The latter takes into account the relative importance of each observation.

**Simple arithmetic mean** For this calculation each item within the group is assumed to have equal importance. The formula for calculating the simple arithmetic mean is given by:

$$\text{a.m.} = \frac{\Sigma x}{n}$$

Given a set of $n$ numbers, $x_1, x_2, x_3, \ldots, x_n$, the a.m. is defined as the sum of the numbers divided by $n$. (Sigma ($\Sigma$) is a sign of summation and $\Sigma x$ denotes the sum of all quantities like $x$. The notation for the arithmetic mean, which is usually abbreviated to **the mean**, is $\bar{x}$ when dealing with sample data and $\mu$ when dealing with population (or universe) data.)

The definition given above is appropriate only in the case of unit frequencies. Suppose that the $x$ values are associated with the frequencies $f_1, f_2, f_3, \ldots, f_n$, then the mean $\bar{x}$ is given by:

$$\bar{x} = \frac{f_1 x_1 + f_2 x_2 + f_3 x_3 + \ldots + f_n x_n}{n}$$

$$\bar{x} = \frac{\Sigma f x}{\Sigma f} = \frac{1}{n} \times \Sigma f x$$

**Example**

| Wages | Frequency | |
|---|---|---|
| $x$ | $f$ | $fx$ |
| 5 | 1 | 5 |
| 6 | 3 | 18 |
| 7 | 8 | 56 |
| 8 | 4 | 32 |
| 9 | 2 | 18 |
| 11 | 1 | 11 |
| 12 | 1 | 12 |
| Total | 20 | 152 |

Therefore, $\bar{x} = \dfrac{152}{20} = \$7.60 =$ the mean wage.

**The weighted arithmetic mean** For this calculation each item within the group is assigned a weight proportional to its importance within that group. The formula for calculating the weighted arithmetic mean is given by:

$$\bar{x} = \frac{w_1 x_1 + w_2 x_2 + w_3 x_3 + \ldots + w_n x_n}{w_1 + w_2 + \ldots + w_n}$$

This can be abbreviated to read:

$$\bar{x} = \frac{\Sigma(wx)}{\Sigma(w)} \quad \text{or} \quad \frac{\Sigma(wx)}{n}$$

where $w_1, w_2, \ldots, w_n$ represent the weights actual or estimated, to be applied to the quantities $w_1 x_1, \ldots, w_n x_n$.

**Example**
Oakham Enterprises employs 350 employees, of which 200 are classified as skilled, 100 as semi-skilled and 50 as unskilled. The mean wage for each group is $1200, $1000, and $780, respectively. The personnel manager wishes to calculate the mean wage paid by the company.

If the simple arithmetic mean is used to calculate the mean wage then we have:

$$\bar{x} = \frac{\Sigma(x)}{n}$$

where the variates $x_1$, $x_2$ and $x_3$ are 1200, 1000 and 780, respectively, and $n = 3$, or

$$\bar{x} = \frac{1200 + 1000 + 780}{3} = \$993.33 \text{ per month.}$$

However, this mean wage is not strictly accurate. The variations in wage rates and the number of operatives in each group make it necessary to calculate the mean monthly wage by using the weighted arithmetic mean. The unskilled workers would feel somewhat cheated if they were told that they were, on average, earning \$993 per month! Thus

$$\bar{x} = \frac{\Sigma(wx)}{n}$$

where weights $w_1$, $w_2$ and $w_3$ are 200, 100 and 50, respectively. Note that $n$ no longer represents the number of classes or groups but the total population. Thus

$$\bar{x} = \frac{(200 \times 1200) + (100 \times 1000) + (50 \times 780)}{350}$$

$= \$1082.9$ per month.

(The unskilled workers may feel that this is an even more unrepresentative figure of their earnings.)

This example shows that the weighted arithmetic mean is the correct method of calculating the mean when items vary in their importance.

## Advantages and disadvantages of the arithmetic mean

### Advantages
1. It is easy to understand and calculate.
2. It utilizes all the data in the group or class.
3. It is suitable for arithmetic and algebraic manipulation.

### Disadvantage
1. It may give too much weighting to items at the extreme limits of the group to such an extent that it may be questionable whether the mean is actually representative of the data.

When finding the $\bar{x}$ of grouped data, we can find either the mid-point of the class, and multiply it by the frequency ($fx$) or, more easily, assume a mean and work in actual deviations from that mean, as shown in the following example.

### Example
Determine the mean of the following monthly earnings.

| Monthly earnings ($) | No. of people |
|---|---|
| 1275.0 | 22 |
| 1425.0 | 38 |
| 1575.0 | 70 |
| 1725.0 | 66 |
| 1875.0 | 34 |
| 2025.0 | 18 |

First make an educated estimate of the mean, say, $1575.0 in this case. The table may now be written as follows:

| Earnings | Frequency | Deviation from assumed mean | Frequency × deviation |
|---|---|---|---|
| 1275.0 | 22 | − 300.0 | − 6600.0 |
| 1425.0 | 38 | − 150.0 | − 5700.0 |
| 1575.0 | 70 | 0.0 | 0.0 |
| 1725.0 | 66 | + 150.0 | + 9900.0 |
| 1875.0 | 34 | + 300.0 | + 10200.0 |
| 2025.0 | 18 | + 450.0 | + 8100.0 |
| | 248 | | + 28200.0; |
| | | | − 12300.0 |

Therefore, $\bar{x} = \$1575$ (the assumed mean) $+ \dfrac{28200 - 12300}{248}$

$= \$1575 + \$64.11$

$= \underline{\$1639}$ (the true arithmetic mean).

## THE GEOMETRIC MEAN

When the *percentage* change rather than the *actual* change is the important factor, it is necessary to calculate the average using the geometric mean. For example, the retail price index, which is concerned with percentage change within a period, is calculated using the geometric mean.

The geometric mean, $g$, can be expressed as the $n$th root of the product of the $n$ quantities comprising the group.

Symbolically,

$$g = \sqrt[n]{x_1 \cdot x_2 \cdot x_3 \cdot \ldots \cdot x_n}$$

and the weighted geometric mean is

$$g = \sqrt[n]{x_1^{w_1} \cdot x_2^{w_2} \cdot x_3^{w_3} \cdot \ldots \cdot x_n^{w_n}}$$

where  $x =$ the variate,
   $w =$ the weighting factor,
   $\Sigma(w) = n$.

## Advantages and disadvantages of the geometric mean

### Advantages
**1**. It utilizes all the data in the group.
**2**. It is determinate (i.e., it is exact), provided that all quantities are greater than zero.
**3**. It attaches less weight to large items than does the arithmetic mean.
**4**. It has certain properties which make it especially useful when dealing with relative as compared with absolute numbers, i.e., it is especially useful when describing ratios.

### Disadvantages
**1**. It cannot be used when any values are zero or negative.
**2**. It is less easy to use and understand than the arithmetic mean.

### Example
A small engineering factory made net profits of $20 000, $80 000 and $200 000 in 1979, 1980 and 1981 respectively. What was the average rate of growth of the firm's profits?

Using the arithmetic mean,
from 20 to 80 (1979/1980) = 4,
from 80 to 200 (1980/1981) = 2.5.
Therefore, $(4 + 2.5)/2 = 3.25$.
However, this could be misleading for:
$20 000 \times 3.25 = $65 000$ and
$80 000 \times 3.25 = $260 000$.

However, by using the geometric mean $g$ can be recalculated as $g = \sqrt[2]{4 \times 2.5} = \sqrt[2]{10} = 3.162$. Therefore, $20 000 \times 3.162 = $63 240$; $80 000 \cdot 3.162 = $252 960$ (this figure being nearer to the actual final profit).

Similarly, calculation of the arithmetic mean of the actual profit figures would give $300 000/3 which equals $100 000. However, as discussed earlier, extreme values of the variate may significantly affect the arithmetic mean. In this example, the $200 000 in 1981 is tending to "pull up" the mean rather more than the $20 000 in 1979 is pulling it down.

If the geometric mean is calculated using the logarithmic method, which is much easier than using the previous formula, a more realistic figure is obtained.

### The logarithmic method

$$\log g = \sum_{i=1}^{n} \frac{\log x_i}{n}$$

This formula looks complicated, but when translated simply means add up all the logs of the variable values and divide by the number of variable values. For example,

$$\begin{aligned}
\log 20\,000 &= 4.3010 \\
\log 80\,000 &= 4.9031 \\
\log 200\,000 &= 5.3010 \\
\hline
&\phantom{=}\ 14.5051
\end{aligned}$$

Thus, 14.5051/3 equals 4.8350. The antilogarithm of this is 68.4 which, converted to five decimal places, equals \$68 400.

However, the geometric mean is rarely used in practice except in economic statistics, where it is of particular use in the construction of index numbers.

For the sake of completeness, the **harmonic mean** of $n$ numbers, $x_1, x_2, x_3, \ldots, x_n$, is defined as $n$ divided by the sum of the reciprocals of the values. The harmonic mean is also rarely used in practice, but it does, on occasions, provide a more appropriate average.

## THE MEDIAN

The median is that value of the variable which divides the group into two equal parts. It may be defined as the value of the value of the middle item (or the mean of the values of the two middle items) when the items are arranged in an ascending or descending order (**array**) of magnitude (size).

### Example

If a set of *ungrouped* values, 2, 4, 6, 8, 10, 12, 14 and 16, are taken and arranged in ascending order of magnitude, then the median value is the mean of 8 and 10 which equals 18/2, i.e., 9. The formula $(n+1)/2$ gives the position of the median, where $n$ represents the number of observations (i.e., the sum of the frequencies). The formula does not give the median; it tells us how many of the ordered values must be counted before the median is reached. If the frequency is normally distributed then the mean and the median will be the same.

### Advantages and disadvantages of the median

#### Advantages
**1.** It eliminates the effect of extreme values.

**2.** It often corresponds to a definite item in the distribution.

**3.** It is easy to calculate and understand.

**4.** Only the values of the middle items need be known, i.e., the median can still be calculated even if the first and last classes are open-ended and the lower and upper units are unknown.

#### Disadvantages
**1.** If the distribution is irregular, the indication of the median may be indefinite.

**2.** When the items are grouped, it may not be possible for the median to be located exactly.

## Calculating the median of *grouped* data

The median, of data grouped into classes, is found by taking the lower boundary of the class into which the median must fall plus a fraction of its class interval.

## Example

Calculate the median from the following set of grouped, discrete data.

| Output per operative | Frequency | Cumulative frequency |
|---|---|---|
| 50–54 | 4 | 4 |
| 55–59 | 8 | 12 |
| 60–64 | 12 | 24 |
| 65–69 | 18 | 42 |
| 70–74 | 21 | 63 |
| 75–79 | 13 | 76 |
| 80–84 | 7 | 83 |
| 85–89 | 3 | 86 |
| 90–95 | 4 | 90 |

First, the frequency is divided into two equal halves, i.e., $n/2$. Since $n$ equals 90, the median occurs at $90/2$ which equals 45. The 45th item occurs in the class 70–74. So the median must equal $70 + 4 \times (45 - 42)/21 = 70.6$, i.e., the median output per operative (71 units).

## THE MODE

The mode is defined as the variable (or *attribute*) which occurs with the most frequency. It can be applied to both quantitative and qualitative data. For example, if more employees in a firm earn $120 per week than any other figure, then the modal wage rate is said to be $120. To give another example, if more car accidents are due to drunken driving than any other cause, then the modal cause of accidents is drunken driving. The mode is a particularly useful average for discrete series, e.g., the number of people who wear a given shoe size. Consider the manager of a shoe shop – would he reorder shoes from the manufacturer by quoting the mean size, the median size or the modal size? There are, however, many problems in which a mode does not exist or where it is not unique, i.e., where there may be more than one mode, giving rise to multimodal frequency distribution.

Unless the mode is self-evident, it may, in practice, be quite difficult to calculate if some degree of precision is required. The only satisfactory method is to fit a curve to the distribution and determine the highest point of the curve in relation to the independent variable. Much depends on the shape of the distribution and the size of the class interval, and, in many cases, only an approximate modal value can be obtained. Hence, the mode is rarely used in practice.

However, it may be calculated using the following formula.

$$\text{Mode} = L + \left( \frac{fa}{fa + fb} \times CI \right)$$

where $L$ represents the lower limit of the modal group,
      $fa$ represents the frequencies in the group following
      the modal group,
      $fb$ represents the frequencies in the group preceding
      the modal group,
      $CI$ represents the class interval.

### Example

In changing over from a piece-work payment system (i.e., payment in relation to the number of items actually produced) to an inclusive day-rate payment system, many problems are encountered. One of these problems is to ensure that the agreed output units on the new day-rate system reflect the true average figure of output which was being achieved on the old piece-work system.

Data were collected over a period of time for a group of employees from a particular packaging operation. These data are displayed in the following table. From an initial inspection of the data, it is possible to identify the mode as 631. One should consider whether this is accurate or whether the spread of the data is such that the approximation is of little use to management or the unions, both of whom require a more accurate figure if negotiations are to be worth while.

### Frequency of productive outputs

| Output units/hour | Frequency | Output units/hour | Frequency |
|---|---|---|---|
| 600 | 1 | 622 | 7 |
| 602 | 1 | 624 | 7 |
| 604 | 3 | 626 | 9 |
| 606 | 2 | 627 | 8 |
| 608 | 2 | 629 | 10 |
| 609 | 3 | 631 | 16 |
| 611 | 2 | 633 | 7 |
| 613 | 4 | 635 | 6 |
| 614 | 4 | 636 | 5 |
| 615 | 3 | 638 | 4 |
| 617 | 4 | 640 | 2 |
| 618 | 5 | 643 | 2 |
| 620 | 8 | | |

The next stage is to retabulate the data into a grouped frequency table as shown below.

### Grouped frequency table

| Output | No. of operatives | Output | No. of operatives |
|---|---|---|---|
| 600–604 | 5 | 625–629 | 27 |
| 605–609 | 7 | 630–634 | 23 |
| 610–614 | 10 | 635–639 | 15 |
| 615–619 | 12 | 640–644 | 4 |
| 620–624 | 22 | | |

Inspection of this table shows that the modal group is 625–629, and hence $L$, the lower value of the modal group, is 625.

The value of $fa$ is obtained from the frequencies in the group *following* the modal group, i.e. 23. The value of $fb$ is obtained from the frequencies in the group *preceding* the modal group, i.e. 22. The class interval, $CI$, used to group the productive output figures is four. If these values are now substituted into the formula on page 23, then

$$\text{Modal value} = L + \left( \frac{fa}{fa + fb} \times CI \right) = 625 + \left( \frac{23}{23 + 22} \times 4 \right)$$

$$= 627 \text{ units of output.}$$

This is clearly a much more accurate figure than that which might have been obtained from the ungrouped data. In addition, several advantages are also gained by using the mode as a measure of location.

## Advantages and disadvantages of the mode

### Advantages

**1.** It is easy to understand.
**2.** It is not affected by open-ended classes or extreme values.
**3.** It is not necessary to know the values of all the items in the distribution in order to calculate the mode.

### Disadvantage

**1.** Its major **disadvantage** is that, because of its imprecision, its utility in calculations requiring a high degree of accuracy is limited, particularly if the distribution is *multimodal* or widely dispersed.

## INDEX NUMBERS

When we compare two things, in which a *relative* change in one is expressed as a percentage of another, we are constructing an index number. However, index numbers not only express binary comparisons, i.e., comparisons of two things, but they are more often used to express a *comparison in series*. Providing the data is homogeneous, countless numbers of factors can be compared, such as productivity, prices, sales, days lost through sickness, industrial accidents, population changes, usage rates and, of course, the index which is probably best known – the Consumer Price Index (CPI).

An index number is similar to an average in that it condenses a multivariable situation into a single number. The main feature of the index is that once a base index has been established, it may be used to make comparisons with the starting base. Generally, the starting base is given the value of 100; hence, if the current price index number is 132, the initial index has increased by 32 points since the initial index base was established.

A significant and increasingly important use of index numbers is their use as the basis for wage negotiations as well as helping to formulate changes in government economic policy, such as changes in direct and/or indirect taxation.

The Consumer Price Index monitors the percentage change in the spending of a typical family on foods and services. The method of construction and calculation of the CPI can be appreciated by considering a very large and representative "basket" of goods and services in January of each year, and then comparing the cost of this same "basket" in each of the following 12 months. The percentage increase in total cost since January can then be calculated. The "basket" is changed each January to ensure that it is as up-to-date as possible, but the percentage changes in the cost of successive "baskets" are linked together to produce a continuous series of percentage changes since the CPI was created.

### Degree of importance
Some items in the 'basket' account for a much greater percentage of the family budget than others. For example, most households spend far more on bread and meat than they do, say, on soap. Therefore, a 10% increase in the cost of bread will clearly add more to the cost of the 'basket' than a 10% increase in the cost of soap. To allow for this *relative* importance of the various items in the 'basket', each percentage change in price is given a **weight** to represent its relative importance in the household expenditure of the previous 12 months. The percentage changes in prices are then multiplied by these weights before being averaged.

### Use of Index Numbers
Let us assume that the current Consumer Price Index is reset at 100. At a later date – four months – and assuming that the contents, services and quantities of the "basket" remain unchanged, the new index figure can then be calculated in the following manner.

$$\text{Index} = \frac{\text{Current total price}}{\text{Original base index figure}} \times 100$$

or

$$\text{Index} = \frac{\Sigma p_n}{\Sigma p_0} \times 100$$

This gives a simple aggregative index.

To calculate an index by a weighting method use the following steps:

**1.** Decide the items to be used in the index and their respective quantities and price per unit.

**2.** Calculate the total cost for each item in the index.

**3.** Sum the total cost column to give the current total cost.

**Example**

The Consumer Price Index for a hypothetical family is given below for 1980, with the 1981 prices shown in brackets.

| Item | Quantity | Unit price $ | Total expenditure $ |
|------|----------|--------------|---------------------|
| Meats | 4 lb | 2.90(3.20) | 11.60(12.80) |
| Vegetables | 4 lb | 0.10(0.12) | 0.40(0.48) |
| Fish | 1.5 lb | 1.90(2.20) | 2.85(3.30) |
| Gas | 45 gal | 0.34(0.38) | 15.30(17.10) |
| Mortgage | 1 | 100.00(90.00) | 100.00(90.00) |
| Energy | 1 | 12.00(15.00) | 12.00(15.00) |
| Appliances | 1 | 3.80(4.60) | 3.80(4.60) |
| Services | 1 | 9.80(10.40) | 9.80(10.40) |

|  |  |  | 155.75(153.68) |

The 1980 figure of 155.75 is therefore given an index base of 100, using the formula:

$$\frac{153.68}{155.75} \times 100 = 98.9.$$

Note that the base year quantities, i.e., those for 1980, are used as weights to obtain the *weighted aggregative index*, or

$$\text{Weighted Index} = \frac{\Sigma p_n'' q_0}{\Sigma p_0 q_0} \times 100$$

where $q_0$ denotes the base year quantities.

**Problems associated with weights and Indeces**

Although the Consumer Price Index should not, strictly speaking, be treated as a cost of living index, since the cost of living is determined essentially by an individual's idiosyncracies and personal expenditure, the CPI is widely used in salary and wage negotiations. A main concern of union negotiators is that the weights in the index may or may not reflect the expenditure patterns of their members. For instance, if an item is weighted less than an individual spends proportionately on it, and the price of that item increases more rapidly than the others in the index, the effect will be less on the index than it will be on their member's wage packet. Thus, a man taking home $300 per week (net) with a total accommodation cost of $60 (20 %) would, in index language, weight his expenditure on housing at 200 (total weights in the index = 1000). If we assume that the weight given to housing in the current year index is 130 or 13 % then this is equivalent to $39 in the member's take home pay, yet he is spending $60 on this item. If total housing costs were to increase by, say, 25 % it would mean that an extra $15 would have to be found by this individual – a cost of living increase of 5 %. The Consumer Price Index would show an increase of only:

$$\frac{130}{1000} \times \frac{25}{100} = 3\%.$$

Although it is not a simple task to construct an index which realistically corresponds to a particular group, it is not too difficult to consider the weights in the groups which comprise the CPI and the price changes of the items concerned, and to make some judgment about the appropriateness of an increase in the CPI. While it may be argued that future price increases cannot be predicted with absolute accuracy, there remains a need (from a negotiator's viewpoint) to make predictions of future increases. The use of **trend analysis techniques** is becoming increasingly important. One such method is that of moving averages.

## MOVING AVERAGES

A moving average may be defined as the average of a consecutive set of $n$ observations, where $n$ is some convenient number. If trends are to be detected or an interest is shown in the general pattern of growth of some particular factor, then a moving average (which is an artificially constructed time series) may well be easier to understand and construct than mathematical equations of time series.

In a moving average each annual (or monthly, weekly or even hourly) figure is replaced by the mean of both itself and those values corresponding to a number of preceding and succeeding periods. In a five-year moving average, each annual figure is replaced by a mean which is calculated by adding the value of the *year under examination*, those values of the two *preceding years* and those values of the two *succeeding years*. The longer the period of time over which the average is calculated, the smoother the curve will be when a number of these averages are plotted against the time scale. Essentially, a moving average tends to 'smooth out' the peaks and valleys which occur as a result of cyclical, seasonal or other periodic variations. The factor under consideration might be profit, turnover or sales per employee, production levels or hospital bed utilization – in fact almost anything which can be quantified and not necessarily on an annual basis. The greater the value of $n$, the smoother the graph becomes, but with the disadvantage that the indication of the trend becomes less noticeable.

A graph on which a number of variable values are plotted against time is called a **historigram** (i.e., a historical record, not to be confused with a *histogram*).

If the averages are calculated over an even number of periods, say, 8 years or 12 months, then the problem arises that the moving averages will have to be plotted between successive years or months. To overcome this difficulty, it is usual to "center" the values by calculating a two-year moving average, at least initially.

### Example
The directors of the Gorite Motor Company are considering

diversification as part of their corporate strategy. However, they are unsure of the degree of diversification which would be prudent and they therefore wish to have an idea of the trend of their car sales. The following figures are available from which five-year moving averages can be plotted.

| Year | Car sales '000s | Five-year moving total | Five-year moving average |
|------|-----------------|------------------------|--------------------------|
| 1965 | 15.6 | | |
| 1966 | 16.8 | | |
| 1967 | 17.2 | 82.9 | 16.58 |
| 1968 | 17.0 | 85.7 | 17.14 |
| 1969 | 16.3 | 86.2 | 17.24 |
| 1970 | 18.4 | 88.6 | 17.72 |
| 1971 | 17.3 | 89.4 | 17.88 |
| 1972 | 19.6 | 91.5 | 18.26 |
| 1973 | 17.8 | 93.6 | 18.72 |
| 1974 | 18.2 | 96.5 | 19.30 |
| 1975 | 20.7 | 95.2 | 19.04 |
| 1976 | 20.2 | 95.0 | 19.00 |
| 1977 | 18.3 | 94.7 | 18.94 |
| 1978 | 17.6 | | |
| 1979 | 17.9 | | |

The two values at the end of the series are lost, which is a slight disadvantage, particularly when the series is very short.

Figure 6 shows the graph which is produced when the moving average and the original data are plotted against the time.

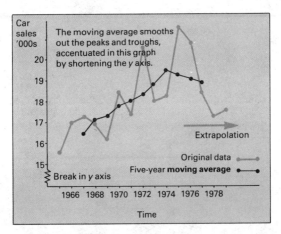

*Figure 6. Gorite five-year moving averages*

Having determined the trend, another technique which can be used in an attempt to predict the values associated with future time periods is that of **extrapolation**. The basic problem associated with extrapolating is in assuming what the prevailing economic forces will be during the period under consideration. However, mathematical models can be built which take **uncertainty** into account. These are discussed more fully in the accompanying book *Operations Research* in this series.

# Chapter 3

# Dispersion

The measures of location – mean, median and mode – which were discussed in the previous chapter provide single numbers which represent whole sets of data. However, a major characteristic of any distribution is its *dispersion* or spread about a central value such as the arithmetic mean. Figure 7 shows that curve A is spread more widely than curve B, although the mean of each distribution is the same.

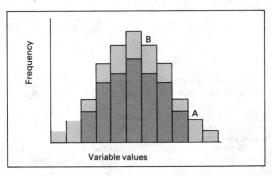

*Figure 7. Dispersion about the same mean*

It is frequently necessary to measure the degree of the dispersion, i.e., to attempt to determine the variability of the population.

### Example

Suppose that a number of people are considering investing in one of three companies and, as one of the criteria of success with which to evaluate the companies, they examine the profile of the market values of the companies' $1.00 nominal value shares, over the past ten years.

| Year | 1 | 2 | 3 | 4 | 5 | 6 | 7 | 8 | 9 | 10 |
|------|------|------|------|------|------|------|------|------|------|------|
| Co. A | 1.25 | 1.55 | 1.60 | 1.60 | 2.00 | 0.85 | 1.70 | 2.15 | 2.40 | 1.90 |
| Co. B | 1.70 | 1.90 | 3.40 | 2.60 | 1.20 | 0.50 | 0.60 | 0.90 | 2.20 | 2.00 |
| Co. C | 1.10 | 1.20 | 1.30 | 1.50 | 2.00 | 2.00 | 2.00 | 1.90 | 2.00 | 2.00 |

The investors would, of course, be more interested in the relative yield per share rather than just the capital change in the value of the share, as far as their investment decision making is concerned. Even so, the variability of the population is quite significant and provides far more information than just the arithmetic mean, the median or the mode.

The mean market value for the shares of each of these companies is $1.70. However, if the investors are unaware of the spread of the prices, they might believe (at least on this information) that there was little to choose between the companies. With the dispersion known, they would want to know why the shares of Company B have varied from $0.50 to $3.40, or why Company C appears to have been fairly stable over the past five years.

In other words, it is necessary to be able to measure the dispersion around the mean. There are several measures used, in particular:

**1.** The range.
**2.** Quartile measures.
**3.** The mean deviation.
**4.** The standard deviation.

## RANGE

The range is defined as the difference between the extreme values of the variable. In Company A above, the range would be $2.40 - 0.85 = 1.55$; in Company B it would be $3.40 - 0.50 = 2.90$; in Company C, $2.00 - 1.10 = 0.90$. Although the range is easy to determine and to use, it is a poor measure of variability because it accounts only for the two *extreme* values of the data. However, the range does tend to be used in quality control to keep a check on the variability of, say, raw materials.

## MEAN DEVIATION

The mean deviation gives the average of all the deviations from the value of the arithmetic mean. If a set of numbers is taken, $x_1, x_2, x_3, \ldots, x_n$ (where $n$ can be any number), which constitute a sample with a mean $\bar{x}$, the amount by which the sample values depart from the mean can be written as $x_1 - \bar{x}$, $x_2 - \bar{x}, x_3 - \bar{x}, \ldots, x_n - \bar{x}$. These amounts are the deviations from the mean. Calculation of the average of these different deviations gives the mean deviation, with the following formula.

**Mean deviation** $= \dfrac{\sum\limits_{i=1}^{n} (x_i - \bar{x})}{n}$

The plus and minus signs of the deviations are ignored, since it is the absolute values of the numbers that are important, i.e., the size or magnitude of the deviations.

## Example

A biscuit manufacturer uses machines which automatically pack 1 kg. of assorted biscuits. To check the average weight delivered, sample packets are selected at regular intervals from the total population. The mean weight of each sample of ten can be found and the variability of the two machines compared by calculating the mean deviations from the mean of each sample. The results from the two machines are as follows.

M/c A 1020 1030 1025 1040 1005 1010  990 1040 1005  985 (g)
M/c B  980  960 1030 1015  990 1025 1020 1020  985 1025 (g)

**Solution**
The mean weight of each sample is the sum of the variables divided by their respective number. Thus,

Machine A $= 10\,150 \div 10 = \bar{x} = 1015$.
Machine B $= 10\,050 \div\ = \bar{x} = 1005$.

Machine B would appear to be the more accurate of the two. However, the deviations from the mean of Machine A are $5+15+10+25+10+5+25+25+10+30 = 160$;   **mean deviation = 16**.

The deviations from the mean of Machine B are $25+45+25+10+15+20+15+15+20+20 = 210$;   **mean deviation = 21**.

While Machine B appears to pack more closely to the required weight it is, in fact, far more erratic than Machine A. (It should be noted that the sign $\bar{x}$ is used in formulae when dealing with *samples*, but the Greek sign $\mu$ is substituted when determining *population* properties.)

## QUARTILES

**The semi inter-quartile range** or **quartile deviation** gives the average amount by which the two quartiles, $Q_3$ and $Q_1$, differ from the median, i.e.,

$$\text{Quartile deviation} = (Q_3 - Q_1) \div 2.$$

The **quartiles** are closely related to the median, which divides the distribution into two parts, each part containing an equal number of observations. The quartiles divide each of these two halves into two further equal parts. It can best be demonstrated by using a cumulative frequency curve as shown in Figure 8. The quartile deviation is comparatively

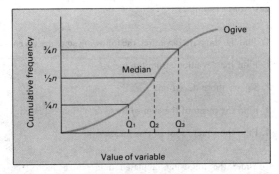

*Figure 8. Determination of the quartiles*

easy to find and it is much more informative than the range. The ogive may be divided into 100 equal parts, each of these divisions being called a **percentile**. ($Q_3$ equals 75 percentiles, the median ($Q_2$) equals 50 percentiles and $Q_1$ equals 25 percentiles.) Percentiles are, however, used rather infrequently.

## STANDARD DEVIATION

**The standard deviation** is a much more useful measure of dispersion than the quartiles, for two main reasons.

**1.** The values of many populations are normally distributed.

**2.** It facilitates comparison between the values of *different* sets of data.

As has already been illustrated by the mean deviation, the extent of the *dispersion* of a given value is shown by the extent of its *deviation* from the mean of the values. In calculating the mean deviation, the signs of the negative deviations were ignored, but this difficulty of signs may be overcome by squaring the deviations. Since all the squared terms will then become positive, the final sum cannot be zero.

The squared deviations are then divided by one less than the number of items, to give the variance. The square root of this is the standard deviation. (Division by $n-1$ instead of $n$ is important when $n$ is small. When $n$ is large, there is little difference.) The formula for this operation may be given as follows:

$$\sigma = \sqrt{\frac{\Sigma f d^2}{n-1}}$$

where $d$ = deviations from the mean,
       $n$ = total number of observations.

(It must be remembered that Greek letters are used for descriptions of populations and Roman letters for descriptions of samples.)

To find the standard deviation, the following steps are taken.

**1.** Find the deviations from the mean.

**2.** Square those deviations.

**3.** Find the mean of the sum of these deviations squared.

**4.** Find the square root of this mean.

Consider the following tabulated data which shows the weekly expenditure on food for 130 households.

| Variable value (x) | Frequency (f) | Frequency × variable (fx) | Deviation from mean (d) | d × f | f × d² |
|---|---|---|---|---|---|
| $40 | 10 | 400 | −15 | −150 | 2250 |
| $45 | 15 | 675 | −10 | −150 | 1500 |
| $50 | 25 | 1250 | − 5 | −125 | 625 |
| $55 | 30 | 1650 | — | — | — |
| $60 | 28 | 1680 | 5 | 140 | 700 |
| $65 | 13 | 845 | 10 | 130 | 1300 |
| $70 | 9 | 630 | 15 | 135 | 2025 |
|  | 130 | 7130 | mean = 55 |  | 8400 |

$$\text{Mean} = \frac{\Sigma fx}{\Sigma f} = \frac{7130}{130} = 55.$$

To find the standard deviation:

**1.** Square the deviations      = 8400.
**2.** Find the mean of these
deviations (the variance)      = 8400 ÷ 130 = 64.6.
**3.** Find the square root of
this mean      = $\sqrt{64.6}$ = 8.04.

Therefore, the standard deviation is 8.04.

A shorter method of calculating the standard deviation can be used by *assuming* the mean and then correcting for the actual mean before the final square root is taken.

**Example**
It is required to find the mean and standard deviation of the following data, relating to the number of people per household in a survey of a district.

| Number of people in household (x) | Frequency (f) | fx | x² | fx² |
|---|---|---|---|---|
| 0 | 3 | 0 | 0 | 0 |
| 1 | 10 | 10 | 1 | 10 |
| 2 | 15 | 30 | 4 | 60 |
| 3 | 27 | 81 | 9 | 243 |
| 4 | 36 | 144 | 16 | 576 |
| 5 | 24 | 120 | 25 | 600 |
| 6 | 4 | 24 | 36 | 144 |
| 7 | 1 | 7 | 49 | 49 |
|  | 120 | 416 |  | 1682 |

**1.**      Mean $\bar{x} = \frac{\Sigma fx}{\Sigma f} = \frac{416}{120} = 3.467.$

**2.** The standard deviation formula of the last section is difficult to apply to this data because the mean is not a whole number. An alternative method is to square the $x$ values instead of the deviations and correct for this afterwards. Sum of squared values $= \Sigma f x^2 = 1682$.

**3.** The **variance** is then:

$$\frac{1}{n}(\Sigma f x^2 - n\bar{x}^2) = \frac{1}{120}(1682 - 120 \times 3.467^2) = 1.999.$$

Note that the divisor $1/n$ is used here because the total frequency is large.

**4.**   Standard deviation = square root of variance,
$$= \sqrt{1.999} = 1.414.$$

### Example
This example illustrates the use of **coding**, which simplifies the above procedures.

Find the mean and standard deviation of the following data which relates to the salary of 130 people.

| Salary range | Mid-point $x$ | $y$ | $z$ | $f$ | $fz$ | $fz^2$ |
|---|---|---|---|---|---|---|
| 1 000–2 000 | 1 500 | −6 000 | −6 | 1 | −6 | 36 |
| 2 000–3 000 | 2 500 | −5 000 | −5 | 7 | −35 | 175 |
| 3 000–4 000 | 3 500 | −4 000 | −4 | 11 | −44 | 176 |
| 4 000–5 000 | 4 500 | −3 000 | −3 | 13 | −39 | 117 |
| 5 000–6 000 | 5 500 | −2 000 | −2 | 19 | −38 | 76 |
| 6 000–7 000 | 6 500 | −1 000 | −1 | 20 | −20 | 20 |
| 7 000–8 000 | 7 500 | 0 | 0 | 23 | 0 | 0 |
| 8 000–9 000 | 8 500 | 1 000 | 1 | 13 | 13 | 13 |
| 9 000–10 000 | 9 500 | 2 000 | 2 | 13 | 26 | 52 |
| 10 000–20 000 | 15 000 | 7 500 | 7.50 | 7 | 52.50 | 393.75 |
| 20 000–40 000 | 30 000 | 22 500 | 22.50 | 3 | 67.50 | 1518.75 |
|  |  |  |  | 130 | −23.00 | 2577.50 |

### Construction of the table

**1.** The mid-point of each range is used to determine the mean and standard deviation.

**2.** The $x$ column is first simplified by subtracting some large number from each mid-point (equivalent to using a **working mean**). The number used here is 7500 because it has the largest frequency.

**3.** The $y$ column is simplified further by dividing each value by 1000 (i.e., the $z$ column).

**4.** The mean and S.D. of the $z$ column are now calculated in the usual way.

$$\bar{z} = \frac{\Sigma fz}{\Sigma f} = \frac{-23}{130} = -0.177.$$

Variance of $z = \frac{1}{n}(\Sigma fz^2 - n\bar{z}^2)$,

$$= \frac{1}{130}(2377.5 - 130 \times (0.177)^2) = 19.796.$$

S.D. of $z = \sqrt{19.796} = 4.449.$

**5.** These values are now **decoded** to give the mean and S.D. of the original data.

$$\bar{x} = 1000\bar{z} + 7500,$$
$$= -177 + 7500 = \underline{7323}.$$

In other words, multiply the mean of $z$ by 1000 and then add 7500 – the reverse of steps 2 and 3 above.

$$\text{S.D. of } x = 1000 \times \text{S.D. of } z,$$
$$= \underline{4449}.$$

The working mean of 7500 must not be added onto the standard deviation – it is a measure of *spread* and is unaffected if every observation is reduced by the same number.

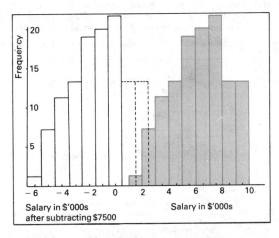

*Figure 9. Distributions with the same standard deviation*

## NORMAL DISTRIBUTION

A distribution which is **symmetrical** about its mean and **bell-shaped** is said to be a normal distribution; occasionally it is also known as a **Gaussian curve**.

In a normal distribution there are proportionately as many *negative* phenomena as there are *positive* phenomena. In other words, the value of y (the frequency) is the same for + x and for − x and therefore the height of the curve, at equal distances on either side of the mean, is the same. (More correctly, the normal curve is symmetrical about the ordinate x = 0.) The curve extends indefinitely in both directions. If the mean (μ) and the standard deviation (σ) of a distribution are known, the height of the curve (y) can be calculated, as can the area under the normal curve. Fortunately, the area under the curve has already been computed and may be found in normal probability tables (see Appendix). If any frequency conforms to a normal distribution pattern, the area under the curve is always divided into certain proportions and, by knowing the standard deviation, it is easy to estimate this proportion (or probability, as the area under the curve equals one).

Below is a list of the percentage area under the curve occupied by a given standard deviation either side of the mean.

    1.00 standard deviations = 68.26 % of the area.
    1.64 standard deviations = 90 % of the area.
    1.96 standard deviations = 95 % of the area.
    2.58 standard deviations = 99 % of the area.
    3.00 standard deviations = 99.75 % of the area.

It should be noted that the normal tables give the area under the curve up to the standard deviation in the *positive* direction, but since the curve is symmetrical the value will be the same beyond the standard deviation in the negative direction (see Figure 10).

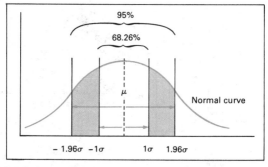

*Figure 10. The normal distribution curve*

In Figure 11, and from tables, two standard deviations above the mean occupy 0.9772 or 97.72 %. Therefore, values greater than 23.00 can be expected in 1 − 0.9772 = 0.0228 (2.28 %) occasions. Equally, the probability of getting a result *smaller* than 17.0 is also 0.0228, and therefore the probability of getting a result *outside the limits* 20 ± 3 is 0.0228 × 2 = 0.0456.

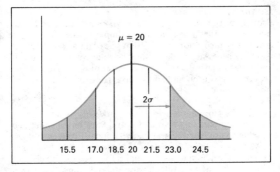

*Figure 11. The normal curve for $\mu = 20$ and $\sigma = 1.5$*

### Example

A retailing company has ten shops, of the same size and sited in similar places in different towns, in an area approximately 80 miles square. The goods sold are perishable and the shops are each supplied once a week from a main depot. At the end of each week, stock remaining has to be written off, as it is uneconomic to return it or dispose of it over the counter. Weekly sales per employee in a test period of five weeks are recorded with the results below (to the nearest multiple of $5).

**1.** Calculate the mean overall weekly sales per employee, assuming that all branches have the same number of employees.

**2.** Given that the standard deviation is $7.7, calculate the range within which 95% of sales per employee should fall. Note that the distribution is approximately normal about the mean. Is such a range consistent with the data?

| Sales per employee ($) | Number of occasions with that level of sales |
|---|---|
| 60 | 2 |
| 65 | 4 |
| 70 | 8 |
| 75 | 15 |
| 80 | 10 |
| 85 | 7 |
| 90 | 3 |
| 95 | 1 |

### Solution

**1.** Using the formula $\dfrac{\Sigma fx}{\Sigma f}$ gives $\bar{x} = \$76.5$

**2.** 95% equals 1.96 standard deviations, which in this case equal $15.09. With a mean of $76.50, 95% of the sales lie between $76.5 ± $15.09 which equals $61.41 to $91.59 and appears to be consistent with the data given in the problem.

## Comparing dispersions

Providing the distributions are of the same kind and measured in the same units, it is a simple process to compare the relative dispersions of different sets of data. To do this, it is simply necessary to determine the ratio between the mean and the standard deviation of each set of data. This simple procedure has been named the **coefficient of variation**.

## Example

The Parks Commission in New York City is considering landscaping part of a lawn in Central Park but is undecided whether to use Norwegian Pine or Douglas Fir trees. It does, however, know that the height of Norwegian Pine has a $\mu$ of 31 m and a $\sigma$ of 3 m while a Douglas Fir has a mean height of 36 m with a $\sigma$ of 4 m. Which variety should the Commission plant to gain uniform overall height?

(CoV = S.D. ÷ mean.)

$$\text{Norwegian Pine} = \frac{3}{31} = 0.097.$$

$$\text{Douglas Fir} \quad = \frac{4}{36} = 0.111.$$

The Norwegian Pine, although generally lower in height, will give a more uniform skyline.

## Skewness

If a unimodal distribution is symmetrical, i.e., a normal curve, then the mean, the median and the mode will all have the same value. If the curve is *not* symmetrical it is said to be **skewed**. A distribution is said to be **negatively skewed** when its peak is to the right, and **positively skewed** when its peak is to the left. The numerical differences between the mean, the median and the mode form the basis for determining the degree of skewness.

# Chapter 4

# Probability

The laws of probability form the basis of nearly all statistical theory. Decision making under conditions of uncertainty must take account of the probabilities of the various outcomes. In spite of the fact that many phenomena are random, the study of probability can help in predicting the most likely overall picture of a situation. For example, the exact time of arrival of a customer in a supermarket is subject to uncertainty, but by analyzing the queuing problem (see *Operations Research* in this series) in terms of the outcome of a large number of events – the arrivals and departures – the most efficient type of service can be determined.

Probability is a measure of the **likelihood** of an event occurring. It always takes values in the range 0 to 1, zero corresponding to **impossibility** and one to **certainty**. For example, it is impossible for a bachelor to be married (by definition), which may be expressed as $P$(bachelor is married) $= 0$. Here the letter $P$ is used as shorthand for "the probability of". For example, it is certain that Washington is the capital of the U.S., expressed as $P$(Washington is the capital of the U.S.) $= 1$.

These are examples of *absolute* impossibility and certainty, i.e., the statements are true or false by definition or by factual content. For future events, it is virtually certain that the sun will rise tomorrow, although some people could argue that it should have a probability very close to one, but not exactly one because it might not happen!

In practice, values of zero and one are rarely encountered, most events being uncertain to a greater or lesser extent. Thus, a *probable* event will have a probability close to one, and an *improbable* event, a probability close to zero. Probabilities may be broadly classified under three headings.

### Theoretical probability
If a card is drawn at random from a deck of cards, it may be concluded, by reference to symmetry, that $P$(ace is drawn) $= 4/52 = 1/13$ because there are 52 cards in the deck, of which 4 are aces.

### Statistical probability
A baker wishes to estimate the probability of a demand of between 100 and 110 loaves. Theoretical considerations offer no help in this case, but an investigation of past records reveals that this demand has been realized on 17 days out of the last 100 days. Thus, $P$(demand between 100 and 110) $= 17/100 = 0.17$. Obviously, this probability will be constantly updated as more past data become available.

### Subjective probability
The chances of the Democrats winning the next presidential election would be considered by some to be very difficult to

assess. A theoretical estimate, based on the fact that there are two major parties, and therefore $P$(Democrats winning) $= 1/2$ will be rejected on the grounds that the parties do not have equally likely chances of winning. Statistical considerations of past elections may be similarly rejected on the ground that the data is irrelevant to the current situation. Public opinion polls are notoriously susceptible to changing attitudes and are only reliable close to the day of the election. Alternatively, a subjective estimate may conclude that $P$(Democrats winning) $= 0.6$, a measure of the individual's degree of belief or strength of conviction.

The *limitation* of this method of assigning measures is that another person might well assign a much lower probability to a particular event (especially, in this case, if he is a keen Republican). Subjective estimates are still useful in business applications, but a consensus from experts must be reached before any reliability can be given to the estimate. For example, oil companies need to determine the chances of a particular field being rich in oil and/or gas. They may well be satisfied with a subjective (but expert) estimate of the probabilities.

### Definition
For **simple** events, the probability may be defined as:

$$\frac{\text{Number of equally likely favorable outcomes}}{\text{Total number of equally likely possible outcomes}}$$

### Example
A promotion campaign offers a first prize of a car in a lottery competition. There are 1000 tickets available and a certain person receives five of them. Then $P$(winning the car) $= 5/1000 = 1/200$ because there are 1000 possible outcomes and five of these outcomes are favorable. Note the importance of the phrase "equally likely" in the definition above. If one of the tickets had been omitted from the draw or if the selection of the winning ticket was not made at random, the probability given above would be erroneous.

**Note** Probabilities are usually expressed as decimals, fractions or percentages. If the **odds** of an event are quoted as 5–2, this represents a probability of $2/7$, i.e., five outcomes are unfavorable while two are favorable, giving a total of seven outcomes. The use of odds will not be used further in this book because betting odds are *not* probabilities. For example, a horse which is quoted at 7-1 against in a race does not have a probability of $1/8$ of winning. Here the odds represent the intention of the bookmaker to pay back seven times the stake, plus the stake, if the horse wins.

## LAWS OF PROBABILITY

Once the probabilities of simple events have been determined, the probabilities of **compound events** can then be calculated according to the following laws.

### Complementary events
If the probability of rain tomorrow is 0.7, then the probability

of no rain tomorrow will be $1.0 - 0.7 = 0.3$. In general, if $A$ stands for the occurrence of an event, then its **complement**, $\bar{A}$, represents the non-occurrence of the event. The first law of probability can be written as:

$$P(\bar{A}) = 1 - P(A) \quad \text{or} \quad P(A) + P(\bar{A}) = 1.$$

In other words, the probability of $A$ not happening is one minus the probability of it happening.

## Simple addition law

Given that the probabilities of a line containing 0, 1, 2 and 3 customers are 0.4, 0.3, 0.2 and 0.1 respectively, then

$P(1 \text{ or } 2 \text{ customers in line}) = 0.3 + 0.2 = 0.5$
$P(\text{less than 3 customers in line}) = P(0 \text{ or } 1 \text{ or } 2 \text{ in line})$
$\qquad\qquad\qquad\qquad\qquad\qquad = 0.4 + 0.3 + 0.2 = 0.9$

In other words, the probabilities are added. This law only applies to **mutually exclusive events**, i.e., events which cannot possibly happen together. The four events in this example are said to be **exhaustive** because the sum of the four probabilities is exactly one, i.e., no other events (numbers in the line) are possible here. In general,

$$P(A \text{ or } B) = P(A) + P(B)$$

when the two events, $A$ and $B$, are mutually exclusive.

## Simple multiplication law

Two events are said to be **independent** when the occurrence or non-occurrence of one of them does not affect the probability of the other occurring. For example, throwing a six with a die and drawing a spade from a deck of cards are independent events because the score on the die does not, even partially, determine the card drawn. In this case $P(6 \text{ on die}) = 1/6$, $P(\text{spade}) = 13/52 = 1/4$ and the probability of both of them occurring is given by $P(6 \text{ on die and spade}) = 1/6 \times 1/4 = 1/24$, i.e., the probabilities are multiplied. In general,

$$P(A \text{ and } B) = P(A) \times P(B)$$

when the events, $A$ and $B$, are independent. A test for statistical independence is given on page 90.

## Example

A machine can malfunction owing to any one of three kinds of potential fault – electrical, mechanical or operational – with probabilities of 2%, 1% and 0.5% respectively. Assuming that the types of failure are independent, calculate the probability that the machine will not function properly.

*Solution*
In this example, the machine can fail to function for a variety of reasons – mechanical failure alone, mechanical and electrical failure, electrical failure only, etc. It will be much easier to calculate the probability that the machine works.

$P$(no mechanical failure) $= 1 - 0.02 = 0.98$.
$P$(no electrical failure) $= 1 - 0.01 = 0.99$.
$P$(no operational failure) $= 1 - 0.005 = 0.995$.

Therefore, $P$(machine works) $= 0.98 \times 0.99 \times 0.995 = 0.9653$ (by independence and the multiplication law).
Therefore, $P$(machine fails) $= 1 - 0.9653 = 0.0347$ (or $3.47\%$).

### Example
Three fair dice are thrown. Find the probability of obtaining at least one 6.

*Solution*
Again, it is simpler to calculate the inverse probability. The complement of at least one 6 is no 6s.

$P$(not a 6 on a die) $= 5/6$.
Therefore, $P$(no 6s on three dice) $= 5/6 \times 5/6 \times 5/6$ $= 125/216$ (by the simple multiplication law).
Therefore, $P$(at least one 6) $= 1 - 125/216 = 91/216$.

### Example
Find the probability of being dealt three aces in a hand (three cards dealt to each person).

*Solution*
$P$(first card is an ace) $= 4/52$.
$P$(second card is an ace) $= 3/51$ because there are only 51 cards left in the deck, of which 3 are aces (assuming the first card was an ace).
Similarly, $P$(third card is an ace) $= 2/50$.
Therefore, $P$(all three cards are aces)
$$= 4/52 \times 3/51 \times 2/50 = 0.000\,181.$$
*Note* $P$(all cards are Kings) $= 0.000\,181$.
       $P$(all cards are Queens) $= 0.000\,181$, etc.
Therefore, $P$(all cards of same type)
$= 0.000\,181 + \ldots + 0.000\,181 = 13 \times 0.000\,181 = 0.002\,35$.

### General addition law
When the events are not mutually exclusive, the simple addition law does not apply. For example, let $A$ represent the drawing of an ace from a deck of cards and let $B$ represent the drawing of a heart when a single card is chosen at random. Then, by counting the possibilities:

$P(A) = 4/52$; $P(B) = 13/52$.
$P(A$ and $B) = 1/52$, i.e., the Ace of Hearts is drawn.
$P(A$ or $B) = 16/52$, i.e., the 13 hearts and the 3 other aces.

Here, the event $A$ or $B$ includes the possibility of *both* $A$ and $B$ occurring. Note that $P(A$ or $B)$ is not the sum of $P(A)$ and $P(B)$ because the Ace of Hearts must only be counted once. The general law is:

$P(A$ or $B) = P(A) + P(B) - P(A$ and $B)$,
i.e., $16/52 = 4/52 + 13/52 - 1/52$.

This equation reduces to the simpler addition law when the variables are mutually exclusive because in such a case $P(A \text{ and } B) = 0$, since $A$ and $B$ cannot happen together.

## CONDITIONAL PROBABILITY

A survey of 100 people reveals the following taste preference for a particular product.

|  | Like | Dislike | Totals |
|---|---|---|---|
| Males | 30 | 20 | 50 |
| Females | 40 | 10 | 50 |
| Totals | 70 | 30 | 100 |

This is an example of a $2 \times 2$ **contingency table** representing a two-way (**dichotomy**) classification of each of the two factors – sex and preference. Using $M$, $F$, $L$ and $D$ to represent male, female, like and dislike the following probabilities can be deduced.

$$P(M) = 50/100 = 1/2; \quad P(F) = 50/100 = 1/2;$$
$$P(L) = 70/100 = 7/10; \quad P(D) = 30/100 = 3/10.$$

But, $P(M \text{ and } L) = 30/100 = 3/10$ which is not the same as $P(M) \times P(L)$.

The reason for this is that the two factors are *not* independent – males are less likely to prefer the product than females. To quantify this difference, the notion of *conditional probability* is introduced. **Given** that a person is male, the probability that he will like the product is $30/50 = 3/5$. This is written as $P(L/M) = 3/5$, pronounced 'the probability of $L$ given $M$'. Similarly, the following conditional probabilities can also be deduced: $P(L/F) = 40/50 = 4/5$; $P(M/L) = 30/70 = 3/7$ because, of the 70 people who like the product, 30 are male.

### General multiplication law

In the above example,

$$P(M \text{ and } L) = P(M) \times P(L/M),$$
i.e., $3/10 \quad = 1/2 \times 3/5$.
Alternatively, $P(M \text{ and } L) = P(L) \times P(M/L),$
i.e., $3/10 = 7/10 \times 3/7$.

In general, $P(A \text{ and } B) = P(A) \times P(B/A) = P(B) \times P(A/B)$, i.e., the probability of $A$ and $B$ is the probability of $A$ multiplied by the probability of $B$ given $A$, or the probability of $B$ multiplied by the probability of $A$ given $B$. When the two events are independent, $P(A/B)$ is the same as $P(A)$, i.e., $B$ is irrelevant to the occurrence of $A$ and the above equation reduces to the simple multiplication law.

### Example

A quality control procedure tests all components coming off a production line. It is found that 5% of the items are defective. The inspection can detect a faulty component with a probability of 98 % but, in 10 % of cases, will classify a good component as being faulty. Find the proportion of components classified correctly.

*Solution*
A faulty component may be represented by $F$, a good one by $G$, a correct classification by $C$ and an incorrect one by $I$. The following probabilities can be deduced.

$$P(F) = 0.05, \ P(G) = 0.95.$$
$$P(C/F) = 0.98, \text{ hence } P(I/F) = 0.02.$$
$$P(I/G) = 0.1, \text{ hence } P(C/G) = 0.9.$$

By the multiplication law.

$$P(F \text{ and } C) = P(F) \times P(C/F) = 0.05 \times 0.98 = 0.049.$$
$$P(G \text{ and } C) = P(G) \times P(C/G) = 0.95 \times 0.9 = 0.855.$$

A correct classification is made in either of these two cases, so the probability of a correct decision is $0.855 + 0.049 = 0.904$.

## TREE DIAGRAMS

A simpler diagrammatic approach to the above problem is to use a tree diagram as in Figure 12.

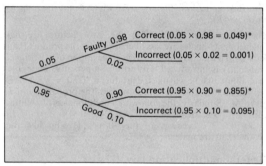

*Figure 12. A tree diagram*

Each component can either be faulty or good and then correctly or incorrectly classified. The probabilities are shown along each branch and add up to one in each of the three pairs. The probabilities along each path are first *multiplied* together to give the probabilities of the four possible compound events. As a check to the arithmetic, these should always add up to one. The cases of correct classification are asterisked in the diagram and *adding* their probabilities together gives the answer to the problem.

## BAYES THEOREM

Three machines, $A$, $B$ and $C$, produce 60 %, 30 % and 10 % respectively of a factory's daily output of precision-made parts. The proportion of components which exceed the tolerance limits varies from machine to machine. 1% of machine A's daily output has to be rejected and, for B and C, the corresponding percentages are 5% and 10%. A component is checked and found to be too large. What is the probability that it was produced by Machine A?

The *a priori* (initial) probability of the component being produced by Machine A is $P(A) = 0.6$ because 60% of all components are made by this machine. On the other hand, Machine A is the most efficient of the three machines and does not produce many rejects. These two facts have somehow to be balanced to give an *a posteriori* (final) probability of $P(A/d)$, where $d$ represents the event of a faulty part being produced. The following tree diagram can be used.

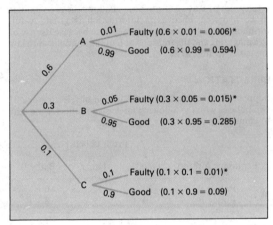

*Figure 13. A tree diagram of faulty components*

A faulty component is produced in each of the three asterisked cases. Hence,

$$P(d) = 0.006 + 0.015 + 0.010 = 0.031.$$

Also, $P(A \text{ and } d) = 0.006$ (the top path in the diagram).

By the multiplication law,

$$P(A \text{ and } d) = P(d) \times P(A/d),$$

i.e., $P(A/d) = \dfrac{P(A \text{ and } d)}{P(d)}$

$$= \frac{0.006}{0.031} = \frac{6}{31} = 0.194 \text{ to three decimal places}$$

Although Machine A produces most components, its efficiency has reduced the probability of it producing the faulty component from 0.6 *a priori* to 0.194 *a posteriori*. The additional information that the component is faulty has produced a change in the assumption that Machine A was the culprit. Similarly,

$$P(B/d) = \frac{P(B \text{ and } d)}{P(d)} = \frac{0.015}{0.031} = \frac{15}{31} = 0.484 \text{ (to 3 d.p.)}$$

and

$$P(C/d) = \frac{P(C \text{ and } d)}{P(d)} = \frac{0.01}{0.031} = \frac{10}{31} = 0.323 \text{ (to 3 d.p.)}$$

From the three *a posteriori* probabilities, Machine B is the most likely one to have produced the faulty component. This is the point of **Bayes theorem** – it allows the probabilities to be reviewed when extra information is given. A full formula for the theorem is not given here because the use of tree diagrams and the transposition of the multiplication law are easier to follow.

## EXPECTATION

Suppose that a company has the option of selecting one of two policies with the following forecasted profits for the year to come.

| Economic forecast | Profit ($'000s) | | |
|---|---|---|---|
| | Good | Fair | Bad |
| Policy *A* | 20 | 12 | 0 |
| Policy *B* | 10 | 9 | 8 |

The estimated probabilities of the economy being good, fair or bad are 0.2, 0,5 and 0.3 respectively. Which policy should the firm adopt? Decision making is facilitated by calculating the expected or average profit in each case.

**Expected value** of Policy *A*
$= 0.2 \times 20 + 0.5 \times 12 + 0.3 \times 0 = 10.$

**Expected value** of Policy *B*
$= 0.2 \times 10 + 0.5 \times 9 + 0.3 \times 8 = 8.9.$

Policy *A* is to be preferred on this basis.

The use of expected values does have certain disadvantages. The firm may be unwilling to allow the possibility of zero profits and on this basis might decide to adopt a *minimax* approach (see *Operations Research* in this series), i.e., maximize the minimum possible profits in each of the two policies. This would mean that Policy *B* would be selected because a profit of at least $8000 is then guaranteed. The method of **expected values** is, nevertheless, a very useful tool as long as the risks involved in its use are appreciated.

**Information** Suppose that, in the last example, a firm of consultants is able to predict exactly the state of the economy for the year ahead. What amount of money would the firm be willing to pay for such information?

| Economy | Policy chosen | Profit | Probability |
|---|---|---|---|
| Good | A | 20 | 0.2 |
| Fair | A | 12 | 0.5 |
| Bad | B | 8 | 0.3 |

The original probabilities have to be used to calculate the expected profit because the firm does not yet know the decision of the consultants. Expected profit with perfect information:

$$= 0.2 \times 20 + 0.5 \times 12 + 0.3 \times 8 = 12.4.$$

This third profit figure exceeds the previous ones by $2400. This value is called the **value of perfect information**. If the consultant's fees are less than this value then the consultants are worth employing; if the fees are exactly $2400, it does not matter whether they are consulted or not.

In practice, information is never perfect, but the problems associated with **imperfect information** (which may, nonetheless, be valuable) are beyond the scope of this book.

### Example

A baker must decide how many rolls to make each day. The rolls cost $0.15 each to make and are sold for $0.30 each. Unsold rolls are sent to a farm, for the pigs, and in this case the baker receives $0.05 per roll, but the baker estimates that unsatisfied demand costs him $0.04 per roll in loss of future business. From past statistics, the daily demand can be summarized as follows:

| Demand | 250 | 260 | 270 | 280 | 290 | 300 |
|---|---|---|---|---|---|---|
| Probability | 0.1 | 0.1 | 0.2 | 0.3 | 0.1 | 0.1 |

Determine the optimum number of rolls the baker must produce in order to maximize profits.

*Solution*
The various options are shown in the following table for a production level of 280 rolls per day.

| De-mand | Number Sold | Number Unsold | Un-satisfied Demand | Conditional Profit ($) |
|---|---|---|---|---|
| 250 | 250 | 30 | 0 | 34.50 |
| 260 | 260 | 20 | 0 | 37.00 |
| 270 | 270 | 10 | 0 | 39.50 |
| 280 | 280 | 0 | 0 | 42.00 |
| 290 | 280 | 0 | 10 | 41.60 |
| 300 | 280 | 0 | 20 | 41.20 |

The **conditional profit** in each row is calculated by finding the return – number sold $\times 0.30$ + number unsold $\times 0.05$ – and subtracting the cost – number made $\times 0.15$ + unsatisfied demand $\times 0.04$. The expected profit when 280 rolls are made is then

$$0.1 \times 34.50 + 0.1 \times 37.0 + 0.2 \times 39.50 + 0.3 \times 42.0 +$$
$$0.2 \times 41.60 + 0.1 \times 41.20 = \$40.09$$

The calculations for the remaining possible production levels are omitted, but they are summarized below.

| Production | 250 | 260 | 270 | 280 | 290 | 300 |
|---|---|---|---|---|---|---|
| Expected profit ($) | 36.42 | 38.03 | 39.35 | 40.09 | 39.96 | 39.25 |

The bakery should produce 280 rolls per day with a maximum expected profit of $40.09.

## DECISION TREES

An oil company wishes to determine whether a particular location is worth drilling or not. The cost of actual drilling is $30000 and the cost of a preliminary survey to assess the chances of oil being present is $20000. There are three basic types of yield:

| A | High yield | Expected income | $800 000 |
|---|---|---|---|
| B | Fair yield | Expected income | $400 000 |
| C | Poor yield | Expected income | 0 |

The preliminary survey is not foolproof and past surveys reveal the following predictions about sites which were eventually drilled.

| | | Actual type of site | | | Total |
|---|---|---|---|---|---|
| | | A | B | C | |
| | A | 6 | 4 | 5 | 15 |
| Predicted type of site | B | 3 | 12 | 5 | 20 |
| | C | 1 | 4 | 20 | 25 |
| | Total | 10 | 20 | 30 | 60 |

For example, at three sites, the survey predicted a B-type field when it was in fact an A-type field. Of forty further sites, which were surveyed but never drilled, the initial investigation predicted that 20 were B-type and 20 were C-type fields.

Determine the optimum decision procedure for the exploitation of the location under consideration, assuming that there is no reason to believe that its geological characteristics are any different from the 100 sites already surveyed.

The possible decisions and outcomes are best illustrated by a **decision tree**.

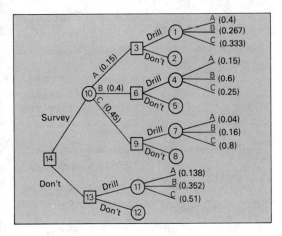

*Figure 14. Decision tree*

Squares have been used to represent **decision nodes** and circles to represent **outcome nodes**. The probability of each branch has to be included after outcome nodes.

For example, after the decision to survey, the probability that a $B$-type field will be predicted is $40/100 = 0.4$ because out of 100 sites surveyed, a $B$ prediction was made 40 times (including the sites never drilled). After the decision to drill, the probability of actually finding an $A$-type field, given that the $B$-type was predicted, is $3/20 = 0.15$, from the second row of the table.

The probabilities in the case of no survey being undertaken include an estimate of the expected number of each type of site in the 40 sites never actually drilled.

|                 |             | $A$ | $B$ | $C$ | Total |
|-----------------|-------------|-----|-----|-----|-------|
| $A$ predicted   | Drilled     | 6   | 4   | 5   | 15    |
| sites           | Not drilled | 0   | 0   | 0   | 0     |
| $B$ predicted   | Drilled     | 3   | 12  | 5   | 20    |
| sites           | Not drilled | 3   | 12  | 5   | 20    |
| $C$ predicted   | Drilled     | 1   | 4   | 20  | 25    |
| sites           | Not drilled | 0.8 | 3.2 | 16  | 20    |
| Total           |             | 13.8| 35.2| 51  | 100   |

In the last row of the table, for example, the proportions of each type of site, of the 20 sites which were predicted as $C$ but never drilled, are the same as those of the 25 sites which were predicted as $C$ and eventually drilled. From the totals row, the probability of finding an $A$-type site is $13.8/100 = 0.138$,

etc. Alternatively, these probabilities can be calculated from
the following tree diagram.

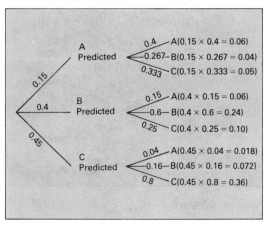

*Figure 15. Tree diagram*

Therefore, $P(A\text{-type}) = 0.06 + 0.06 + 0.018 = 0.138$.
$\qquad\quad P(B\text{-type}) = 0.04 + 0.24 + 0.072 = 0.352$.
$\qquad\quad P(C\text{-type}) = 0.05 + 0.10 + 0.360 = 0.510$.

The expected profits (E.P.) can now be calculated by a
**backward pass** through the tree (in '000 \$):

**Node 1:**
E.P. $= 0.4 \times 800 + 0.267 \times 400 + 0.333 \times 0 = 426.8$.
**Node 2:**
E.P. $= 0$ (no drilling).

Since drilling costs are \$300000 the decision when $A$ is
predicted must be to drill.

**Node 3:**
E.P. $= 426.8 - 300 = 126.8$.
**Node 4:**
E.P. $= 0.15 \times 800 + 0.6 \times 400 + 0.25 \times 0 = 360$.
**Node 5:**
E.P. $= 0$ (no drilling).

Again, it is worth drilling when $B$ is predicted.

**Node 6:**
E.P. $= 360 - 300 = 60$.
**Node 7:**
E.P. $= 0.04 \times 800 + 0.16 \times 400 + 0.8 \times 0 = 96$.
**Node 8:**
E.P. $= 0$ (no drilling).

Here, the E.P. when $C$ is predicted is \$96000 and since the
cost of drilling exceeds this, the decision is made not to drill.

**Node 9:**
E.P. $= 0$.

The E.P. when a survey is made can be calculated from the values of nodes 3, 6 and 9.

**Node 10:**
E.P = $0.15 \times 126.8 + 0.4 \times 60 + 0.45 \times 0 = 43.02$.

**Node 11:**
E.P. = $0.138 \times 800 + 0.352 \times 400 + 0.51 \times 0 = 251.2$.

**Node 12:**
E.P. = 0 (no drilling).

Again, it is not worth drilling without a survey.

**Node 13:**
E.P. = 0.

Finally, the expected payoff can be calculated for Node 14.
Survey: E.P. = $43.02 - 20 = 23.02$ from Node 10.
Don't survey: E.P. = 0 from Node 13.
The decision is to survey.

**Node 14:**
E.P. = 23.02.

**Optimum procedure**
Survey and drill only if $A$- or $B$-types are predicted.
Expected payoff = \$23 020.

## PERMUTATIONS

A personnel manager has to select two candidates from a short list of five, one to be responsible for home sales and the other for foreign sales. In how many ways can the selection be made?

For the first post, the manager may select any one of the five candidates. Having made his choice, he can then choose any of the remaining four. Hence, the total number of possible selections is $5 \times 4 = 20$. Representing the five candidates by the letters A, B, C, D and E, the possible selections are shown below.

| | | | | |
|---|---|---|---|---|
| AB | BA | CA | DA | EA |
| AC | BC | CB | DB | EB |
| AD | BD | CD | DC | EC |
| AE | BE | CE | DE | ED |

Each of these selections is called a *permutation*.

The *order* of the letters is relevant – AB means that A becomes responsible for home sales, whereas BA means that B does. In the above case, the number of permutations of five objects was calculated, taken two at a time, and is written as $P^2_p$.

Thus, $P^2_5 = 20$.
Similarly, $P^2_7 = 7 \times 6 = 42$.
$P^3_7 = 7 \times 6 \times 5 = 210$.
$P^7_7 = 7 \times 7 \times 5 \times 4 \times 3 \times 2 \times 1 = 5040$ (the number of ways of arranging 7 objects in order).

A formula for the number of permutations in the general case can be obtained by introducing the **factorial notation**:

$$1! = 1, \ 2! = 2 \times 1 = 2, \ 3! = 3 \times 2 \times 1 = 6,$$
$$4! = 4 \times 3 \times 2 \times 1 = 24, \text{ etc.}$$

*Note* 0! is defined to be 1 whenever it occurs in a formula.

Then, $\quad P_7^3 = \dfrac{7!}{4!} = \dfrac{7 \times 6 \times 5 \times 4 \times 3 \times 2 \times 1}{4 \times 3 \times 2 \times 1} = 210$ (as before).

and, $\quad P_7^7 = \dfrac{7!}{0!} = \dfrac{7 \times 6 \times 5 \times 4 \times 3 \times 2 \times 1}{1} = 5040.$

In general, $\quad P_n^r = \dfrac{n!}{(n-r)!}$

### Example

A tea-taster has to choose the four best brands from a selection of six types of tea and rank them in order. In how many ways can this be done?

*Solution*

The order is important in this example. The number of permutations $P_6^4 = \dfrac{6!}{(6-4)!}$ by the above formula

$$= \frac{6!}{2!} = \frac{6 \times 5 \times 4 \times 3 \times 2 \times 1}{2 \times 1} = 360.$$

### COMBINATIONS

When the ordering of the selection is *unimportant*, the selection is called a **combination**. Suppose that the tea-taster in the above example has simply to choose the best brands without ranking them. Of the 360 permutations above, the following will be in the list: ABCD, ABDC, ACBD, BDAC, etc. (A–F are the brands), in other words, all the permutations containing the letters A, B, C and D (24 of them). Now each of these is equivalent to the single combination ABCD and, by a similar argument, every other combination will be duplicated 24 times in this manner.

Hence, the number of combinations can be written as:

$$C_6^4 = \frac{360}{24} = 15$$

In general, $\quad C_n^r = \dfrac{n!}{r!(n-r)!} \quad$ i.e. $\quad \dfrac{P_n^r}{r!}$

For example, $\quad C_7^3 = \dfrac{7!}{3!4!} = \dfrac{7 \times 6 \times 5 \times 4 \times 3 \times 2 \times 1}{3 \times 2 \times 1 \times 4 \times 3 \times 2 \times 1} = 35$

and, $\quad C_7^5 = \dfrac{7!}{5!2!} = \dfrac{7 \times 6 \times 5 \times 4 \times 3 \times 2 \times 1}{5 \times 4 \times 3 \times 2 \times 1 \times 2 \times 1} = 21.$

### Example

On a certain Saturday, there were 12 score draws in the

football league out of 60 matches. If a person has to select 8
games from these 60 on his pools forecast, in how many ways
can he select 8 score draws?

*Solution*
Although selections are often called 'perms' in the context of
pools forecasting, it clearly does not matter in which order
the 8 games are chosen. This is a problem about combinations.

$$\text{Total number of selections} = C^8_{60} = \frac{60!}{8!52!}$$

$$= \frac{60 \times 59 \times \ldots \times 1}{8 \times \ldots \times 1 \times 52 \times \ldots \times 1}$$

$$= \frac{60 \times 59 \times 58 \times 57 \times 56 \times 55 \times 54 \times 53}{8 \times 7 \times 6 \times 5 \times 4 \times 3 \times 2 \times 1} \quad \text{(cancelling } 52 \times \ldots \times 1)$$

$= 2\,558\,620\,845$, i.e., roughly 2.5 thousand million combinations.

Total number of ways of selecting 8 score draws from the
12 score draws:

$$= C^8_{12} = \frac{12!}{8!4!} = \frac{12 \times 11 \times \ldots \times 1}{8 \times \ldots \times 1 \times 4 \times \ldots \times 1}$$

$$= \frac{12 \times 11 \times 10 \times 9}{4 \times 3 \times 2 \times 1} \text{ (cancelling } 8 \times \ldots \times 1)$$

$= 495$.

## THE BINOMIAL DISTRIBUTION

The calculation of probabilities involving a large number of
events is very difficult without the notion of combinations.
Suppose that the incidence of occupational disease in a
certain industry is 20% and that it is required to calculate the
probability that two out of four workmen will contract the
disease. Numbering the workmen 1 to 4 and using D for
contracting the disease and N for not contracting it, we have
the following possibilities.

| 1 | Workmen 2 | 3 | 4 | Probability (multiplication law) |
|---|---|---|---|---|
| D | D | N | N | $1/5 \times 1/5 \times 4/5 \times 4/5 = 16/625$ |
| D | N | D | N | $1/5 \times 4/5 \times 1/5 \times 4/5 = 16/625$ |
| D | N | N | D | $1/5 \times 4/5 \times 4/5 \times 1/5 = 16/625$ |
| N | D | D | N | $4/5 \times 1/5 \times 1/5 \times 4/5 = 16/625$ |
| N | D | N | D | $4/5 \times 1/5 \times 4/5 \times 1/5 = 16/625$ |
| N | N | D | D | $4/5 \times 4/5 \times 1/5 \times 1/5 = 16/625$ |

The first row means that workmen 1 and 2 both contract the disease. $P(2$ workmen contract the disease) $= 6 \times 16/625 = 96/625$ because the probabilities have to be *added* together (cf. tree diagrams). An easier approach is to use the fact that the six probabilities are the same and are all equal to $(1/5)^2(4/5)^2$, and the number of ways in which two men contract the disease is $C_4^2 = 6$ (i.e., choosing the two men from four to have the disease).

Thus,        $P(2$ contract the disease)

$$= C_4^2 \times \left(\frac{1}{5}\right)^2 \times \left(\frac{4}{5}\right)^2 = 6 \times \frac{16}{625} = \frac{96}{625}$$

Similarly, $P(0$ contract the disease)

$$= C_4^0 \times \left(\frac{1}{5}\right)^0 \times \left(\frac{4}{5}\right)^4 = 1 \times \frac{256}{625} = \frac{256}{625}$$

$P(1$ contract the disease)

$$= C_4^1 \times \left(\frac{1}{5}\right)^1 \times \left(\frac{4}{5}\right)^3 = 4 \times \frac{64}{625} = \frac{256}{625}$$

$P(3$ contract the disease)

$$= C_4^3 \times \left(\frac{1}{5}\right)^3 \times \left(\frac{4}{5}\right)^1 = 4 \times \frac{4}{625} = \frac{16}{625}$$

and,        $P(4$ contract the disease)

$$= C_4^4 \times \left(\frac{1}{5}\right)^4 \times \left(\frac{4}{5}\right)^0 = 1 \times \frac{1}{625} = \frac{1}{625}$$

*Note* $C_4^0 = \dfrac{4!}{0!4!} = \dfrac{24}{1 \times 24} = 1$ and any number to the power zero is defined to be 1, e.g., $\left(\dfrac{1}{5}\right)^0 = \left(\dfrac{4}{5}\right)^0 = 1$.

In each expression, the power of 1/5 is the number of people with the disease and the power of 4/5 is the number without it. The distribution is graphically represented in Figure 16.

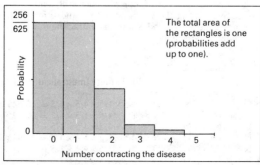

*Figure 16. Binomial distribution*

This is an example of a **discrete probability distribution** – the variable is the number of workmen with the disease and the vertical axis represents *probability* instead of *frequency*.

The particular distribution in this example is called the **binomial distribution** which has the following definition.

In $n$ independent realizations of an event, each of which has probability $p$ of success, probability $q = 1 - p$ of failure, the probability $P(r)$ of obtaining $r$ successes is given by $P(r) = C_n^r p^r q^{n-r}$.

In the example of the workmen, $n = 4$, $p = 1/5$, $q = 4/5$ and a "success" is equivalent to contracting the disease. The events (contracting the disease or not) must be independent. Here, $n$, $p$ and $q$ are called the **parameters** of the binomial distribution.

### Example
The percentage of defective articles produced by a machine is 5%. The articles are packed in boxes of 10. Find the probabilities of the following.

**1.** A box containing no defective articles.
**2.** A box containing three defective articles.
**3.** A box containing more than one defective article.

*Solution*
In this problem, the assumption of independence is justified and $n = 10$, $p = 0.05$ and $q = 0.95$, a "success" being defined as an article that is defective.

**1.** $P(0 \text{ defectives}) = C_{10}^0 \ (0.05)^0 \ (0.95)^{10}$
$\qquad\qquad\qquad\quad = (0.95)^{10}$
$\qquad\qquad\qquad\quad = 0.599$, to three decimal places.

**2.** $P \ (3 \text{ defectives}) = C_{10}^3 \ (0.05)^3 \ (0.95)^7 = 0.010$, to three decimals places, since

$$C_{10}^3 \ = \frac{10!}{3!7!} = \frac{10 \times 9 \times 8}{3 \times 2 \times 1} = 120 \text{ (cancelling } 7!).$$

**3.** If the box contains more than one defective, it can contain $2, 3, \ldots, 9$ or 10 defectives. The direct approach would be to find the probability of each of these events and add them together. Clearly, this will be a very long task and it is easier to find the opposite probability of getting 0 or 1 defectives and deducing the answer from this.

$P(1 \text{ defective}) = C_{10}^1 \ (0.05)^1 \ (0.95)^9 = 10 \times 0.05 \times (0.95)^9$
$\qquad\qquad\qquad\quad = 0.315$, to three decimal places.

$\therefore P \ (0 \text{ or } 1 \text{ defective}) = P(0) + P(1) = 0.599 + 0.315$
$\qquad\qquad\qquad\qquad\qquad = 0.914$, using part **1**.

$\therefore \ P \text{ (more than 1 defective)} = 1 - 0.914,$
$\qquad\qquad\qquad\qquad\qquad\quad = 0.086$, to three decimal places.

(On average, 1 in every 12 boxes is found to be defective.)

## MEAN AND STANDARD DEVIATION

A probability distribution has a mean and standard deviation just as a frequency distribution does. The formulae are:

Mean or expected value $\mu = \Sigma x p(x)$.
Variance $\sigma^2 = \Sigma (x - \mu)^2 p(x)$.

Here, $x$ represents the values of the variable, $p(x)$ the corresponding probabilities and the Greek letters $\mu$ and $\sigma$ are used instead of $\bar{x}$ and $s$ because these are theoretical values.

For the binomial distribution with parameters $n = 4$, $p = 0.25$ and $q = 0.75$, the calculation is given below.

| Number of successes $x$ | Probability $p(x)$ | $xp(x)$ | $x - \mu$ | $(x-\mu)^2$ | $(x-\mu)^2 p(x)$ |
|---|---|---|---|---|---|
| 0 | 81/256 | 0 | $-1$ | 1 | 81/256 |
| 1 | 108/256 | 108/256 | 0 | 0 | 0 |
| 2 | 54/256 | 108/256 | 1 | 1 | 54/256 |
| 3 | 12/256 | 36/256 | 2 | 4 | 48/256 |
| 4 | 1/256 | 4/256 | 3 | 9 | 9/256 |
|  | 1 | 1 |  |  | 192/256 = 0.75 |

The sum of probabilities, $\Sigma p(x)$, is always one for a probability distribution.

Mean $\mu = \Sigma x p(x) = 1$.

Variance $\sigma^2 = \Sigma (x - \mu)^2 p(x) = 0.75$.

Standard deviation $\sigma = \sqrt{0.75} = 0.866$, to three decimal places.

*Note* The expected number of successes in this example can be deduced very easily – if the probability of a success is 0.25 and four trials are made, the average number of successes will be $4 \times 0.25 = 1$.

For the binomial distribution with parameters $n$, $p$ and $q$, it can be proved that

$$\mu = np \quad \text{and} \quad \sigma = \sqrt{npq}.$$

In this example, $\mu = 4 \times 0.25 = 1$ and $\sigma = \sqrt{4 \times 0.25 \times 0.75} = \sqrt{0.75} = 0.866$ as before.

These two formulae are extremely important and will be referred to again in the next chapter.

## POISSON DISTRIBUTION

This distribution is another **discrete** probability distribution and has been found to describe a wide range of random phenomena including the occurrence of accidents or failures, arrivals of calls at a switchboard, arrivals of customers to a check-out line and radioactive disintegrations and emissions.

The distribution is described by the formula:

$$P (x \text{ occurrences}) = e^{-\mu}\left(\frac{\mu^x}{x!}\right) \text{ for } x = 1, 2, 3, 4, \ldots$$

The only **parameter** of the Poisson distribution is $\mu$, which represents the average number of occurrences; e is the **Euler number** and has a value of 2.7182 to four decimal places.

For example, a switchboard receives, on average, two calls per minute. The probabilities of receiving $0, 1, 2, \ldots, 8$ calls in a one-minute interval are shown below using a value of $\mu = 2$ (mean number of calls per minute).

$$P(0 \text{ calls}) = e^{-2}\frac{2^0}{0!} = e^{-2} \times \frac{1}{1} = 0.135.$$

$$P(1 \text{ call}) = e^{-2}\frac{2^1}{1!} = e^{-2} \times \frac{2}{1} = 0.271.$$

$$P(2 \text{ calls}) = e^{-2}\frac{2^2}{2!} = e^{-2} \times \frac{4}{2} = 0.271.$$

$$P(3 \text{ calls}) = e^{-2}\frac{2^3}{3!} = e^{-2} \times \frac{8}{6} = 0.180.$$

$$P(4 \text{ calls}) = e^{-2}\frac{2^4}{4!} = e^{-2} \times \frac{16}{24} = 0.090.$$

$$P(5 \text{ calls}) = e^{-2}\frac{2^5}{5!} = e^{-2} \times \frac{32}{120} = 0.036.$$

$$P(6 \text{ calls}) = e^{-2}\frac{2^6}{6!} = e^{-2} \times \frac{64}{720} = 0.012.$$

$$P(7 \text{ calls}) = e^{-2}\frac{2^7}{7!} = e^{-2} \times \frac{128}{5040} = 0.003.$$

$$P(8 \text{ calls}) = e^{-2}\frac{2^8}{8!} = e^{-2} \times \frac{256}{40\,320} = 0.001.$$

The remaining probabilities gradually get nearer and nearer to zero. Note that $e^{-2} = 1/e^2$.

Graphically, this Poisson distribution has the form shown in Figure 17.

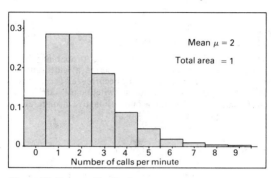

*Figure 17. Poisson distribution*

Using this distribution, the probability of obtaining at least one call in a length of interval of two minutes can be evaluated simply by changing the value of $\mu$.

In one minute, mean number of calls = 2.
In two minutes, mean number of calls = 4, i.e., $\mu = 4$ now.

$$P(0 \text{ calls in two minutes}) = e^{-4}\frac{4^0}{0!} = e^{-4} = 0.018.$$

$$P(\text{at least one call}) = 1 - 0.018 = 0.982.$$

*Note* The standard deviation of a Poisson distribution with parameter $\mu$ is $\sqrt{\mu}$.

### Example
A warehouse finds that, on average, three components of a certain type are required every month. To what level must stock be made up every month in order that there will be a less than 10% chance of running out of stock?

*Solution*
This may be determined by evaluating the **cumulative probabilities**.

| Number required | Probability | Cumulative probability |
|---|---|---|
| 0 | $e^{-3}\dfrac{3^0}{0!} = 0.050$ | $0.050 \; P(0 \text{ needed})$ |
| 1 | $e^{-3}\dfrac{3^1}{1!} = 0.149$ | $0.199 \; P(\leqslant 1 \text{ needed})$ |
| 2 | $e^{-3}\dfrac{3^2}{2!} = 0.224$ | $0.423 \; P(\leqslant 2 \text{ needed})$ |

| Number required | Probability | Cumulative probability |
|---|---|---|
| 3 | $e^{-3}\dfrac{3^3}{3!} = 0.224$ | $0.647\ P(\leqslant 3 \text{ needed})$ |
| 4 | $e^{-3}\dfrac{3^4}{4!} = 0.168$ | $0.815\ P(\leqslant 4 \text{ needed})$ |
| 5 | $e^{-3}\dfrac{3^5}{5!} = 0.101$ | $0.916\ P(\leqslant 5 \text{ needed})$ |

If the warehouse brings stock up to five components every month, the probability of demand exceeding this during the next month is $1 - 0.916 = 0.084$, i.e., $8.4\%$.

## BINOMIAL APPROXIMATION

An insurance company finds that the probability of a person dying within one year is 0.0004. Find the probability that there will be: 0 claims; 5 claims from the 10 000 policy holders during the next year.

This is a binomial distribution with parameters $n = 10\,000$, $p = 0.0004$ and $q = 0.9996$. Therefore,

$P(0 \text{ claims}) = (0.9996)^{10\,000} = 0.018.$
$P(5 \text{ claims}) = C_{10000}^{5}(0.0004)^5(0.9996)^{9995}.$
(The last expression is very difficult to calculate.)

Alternatively, the Poisson distribution can be used as an approximation of the binomial distribution when $n$ is large ($> 100$) and $p$ is small ($< 0.05$).

Mean $\mu = np = 10\,000 \times 0.0004 = 4$ (see page 60).
Therefore, $P(0 \text{ claims}) = e^{-4} = 0.018$. (In fact the approximation is correct to four decimal places.)

$$P(5 \text{ claims}) = e^{-4}\frac{4^5}{5!} = e^{-4} \times \frac{1024}{120} = 0.156.$$

## NORMAL APPROXIMATION TO THE BINOMIAL

The binomial distribution can also be approximated by a normal distribution. This approximation is fairly accurate when $n$ is larger than 20 and $p$ is not too close to 0 or 1. For values of $p$ near to 0 or 1, the value of $n$ has to be larger to remove the *skew* of the binomial distribution. To find the probability of obtaining 55 or more heads when a fair coin is tossed would, for example, be a very time-consuming task if the binomial probabilities had to be used. The normal approximation, however, is simple to apply (see page 60).

$\mu = np = 100 \times 0.5 = 50.$
$\sigma^2 = npq = 100 \times 0.5 \times 0.5 = 25.$
$\sigma = 5.$

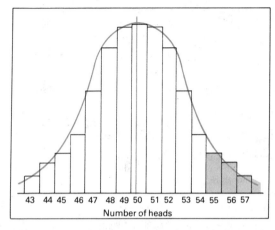

*Figure 18. Normal approximation to the binomial*

The graph shows the binomial distribution with the normal distribution fitted. The shaded area represents the probability of obtaining 55 heads or more. A correction has to be made because the binomial distribution applies to **discrete** variables (the number of heads must be a whole number) whereas the normal distribution applies to **continuous** variables (all values being possible). From the graph, the shaded area begins at 54.5 because the mid-points of each rectangle represent the number of heads.

54.5 is $\dfrac{54.5 - 50}{5} = 0.9$ standard deviations above the mean.

From normal tables,

area up to 0.9 is 0.8159,
∴ area beyond 0.9 is $1 - 0.8159 = 0.1841$,
$P(55$ or more heads$) = 0.1841$.

This approximation will be used in Chapter 5 when hypothesis testing is introduced.

*Note* A similar approximation may be applied to the Poisson distribution when $\mu > 25$. The mean and standard deviation of the approximating normal distribution are $\mu$ and $\sqrt{\mu}$ respectively.

### Example
A telephone exchange deals with an average of 200 calls per minute. However, the maximum number of calls per minute that the exchange can handle is only 190. Find the proportion of the time the system is overloaded.

*Solution*

$$\mu = 200.$$
$$\sigma = \sqrt{200} = 14.14.$$

Using the normal approximation, the results can be seen in Figure 19 below.

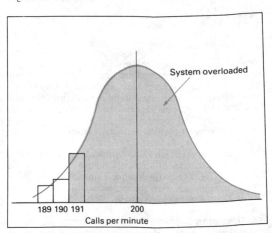

*Figure 19. Normal approximation to the Poisson*

The shaded area represents the probability of 191 or more calls per minute. This area begins at 190.5.

### Standardized normal variate

$$= \frac{190.5 - 200}{14.14} = -0.67.$$

From normal tables the area up to $+0.67$ is 0.7486. By symmetry, this is the same as the shaded area above. Therefore, $P(\text{system overloaded}) = 0.7486 \approx 75\%$.

m is overloaded 75% of the time.

# Chapter 5

# Tests of Significance

Consider the following problem, which is of the type often encountered by a production manager whenever he has to control the quality of his product. Packages produced by a machine have a nominal mean weight of 1.5 lb. with standard deviation 0.005 lb. A package is drawn at random from the production line and found to weigh 1.515 lb. Is there any evidence to suggest that the machine is faulty?

The production manager has to formulate a decision based on the characteristics of a random sample taken from the production line. The above example is simplified because the sample size is one, but the problem will serve as an introduction to significance testing.

**The first step** is to determine the characteristics of the **population** under consideration. Here the population consists of the weights of packages produced by the machine, which may be assumed to have a normal distribution (see page 39) with a nominal mean $\mu = 1.5$ and standard deviation $\sigma = 0.005$. Note that Greek letters are used because *population* parameters are being considered, i.e., characteristics of the population rather than of the *sample*.

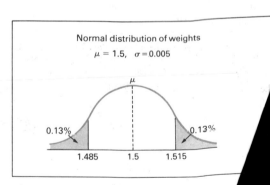

Figure 20. Normal distribution of weights

The sample value of 1.515 is shown in Figure standard deviations from the mean and thi **critical ratio**. It may be calculated fror formula.

Critical ratio $(z) = \dfrac{x - \mu}{\sigma} = \dfrac{1.515 - 1.5}{0.005} =$

(Here $z$ is a variate of the standardized

The area beyond the value 1.515 can be calculated from normal distribution tables. This area is $1 - 0.9987 = 0.0013$, i.e., $0.13\%$. In other words, the probability of obtaining a sample value as high as 1.515 is only $0.13\%$, or 1 in 769 samples. This is a very rare occurrence and the production manager may well decide that the machine is faulty on the basis of this, i.e., that the mean of the population has changed. Care must be taken here for there are other sample weights which might lead to the same conclusion. A value as low as 1.485 is also three standard deviations from the mean but on the other side of the graph. Hence $P$ (of obtaining sample values of more than three standard deviations from the mean) $= 0.26\%$. This is shown as the shaded area in Figure 20. If the sampling procedure was to be repeated it would be found that, on average, only 1 in 385 sample weights would be as far away from the mean as this. It can be concluded, on the evidence of a single weight, that the machine is faulty because the probability is so low.

**The general method** Figure 21 shows the general approach to significance (or **hypothesis**) testing.

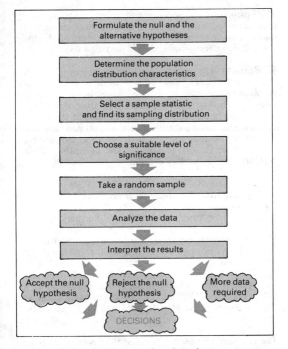

*Figure 21. The general approach to hypothesis testing*

**1. Hypothesis** The problem must be clearly defined before any testing can commence. The assumptions made for the test are contained in the **null hypothesis**. The critical ratio is calculated on the assumption that the population mean is 1.5, i.e., initially it is assumed that the machine is not faulty. The **alternative hypothesis** is that the mean has changed, i.e., the machine is faulty.

## 2. Formulation
**(a)** Null hypothesis: $\mu = 1.5$ (machine is not faulty).
Alternative hypothesis: $\mu \neq 1.5$ (machine is faulty)
Here, $\neq$ means not equal to.

If the production manager had suspicions that the machine was producing overweight packages, he might formulate the problem as follows.

**(b)** Null hypothesis: $\mu = 1.5$ (machine is not faulty).
Alternative hypothesis: $\mu > 1.5$ (the mean has increased).

*Note* that the *simplest* hypothesis is always chosen as the null hypothesis because the value of $\mu$ is needed for the test and the alternative hypotheses do not specify the value of $\mu$, i.e., they simply state that the mean is not 1.5.

**3. Population** The population distribution characteristics are determined in the example by making the assumption that the weights are normally distributed with mean 1.5 lb. (from the null hypothesis) and standard deviation 0.005 lb.

**4. Sample** The sample must be *representative* of the population and sampling must be made *at random*. *Valid* conclusions can only be inferred when *unbiased* data are available. The **sample statistic** is a measure of the sample data. In the introductory example, the sample statistic is a single weight but if a sample of five weights had been taken instead, the obvious sample statistic to use would have been the mean weight of the sample. The **sampling distribution** is the probability distribution of the sample statistic (see page 71).

**5. Significance** The decision to accept or reject the null hypothesis depends upon the likelihood that the value of the sample statistic could have arisen by fluctuations in the random sampling. The probability of 0.26 % on page 67 is the likelihood of obtaining a weight as far from the mean as three standard deviations, on the assumption that the mean of the population is 1.5 lb. It is important to decide how low this probability has to be before rejecting the null hypothesis. Most statisticians use a level of 5 % as the criterion but values as low as 1 % or 0.1 % might be needed if the consequences of the test could be very costly or *crucial* (e.g., in medical research).

The criterion for rejection is called the **level of significance** (or simply **significance level**) of the test. The result of the test is deemed to be **significant** if the probability of the result occurring by chance is lower than the significance level. Alternatively, the test might be described as significant at the 5 % level if this probability is smaller than 5 %.

In practice, the probability is rarely evaluated. For the normal distribution the following **critical values** can be deduced from tables.

5% of the area lies outside the range −1.96 to +1.96.
1% of the area lies outside the range −2.58 to +2.58.
0.1% of the area lies outside the range −3.29 to +3.29.
0.01% lies outside the range −3.89 to +3.89.

From this table, the critical ratio of three, in the introductory example, is significant at the 1% level – the probability of getting a result as far from the mean as this is less than 1% (a highly significant result). On the other hand, a critical ratio of one is likely to occur by chance and is *not* significant. The decision method is shown below.

| Result | Decision |
|---|---|
| Significant at 5% level. | Reject the null hypothesis with reasonable confidence. |
| Significant at 1% level. | Reject with a high degree of confidence. |
| Significant at 0.1% level. | Reject with an extremely high degree of confidence. |
| Not significant. | Accept the null hypothesis. |
| Not significant but close to the 5% level. | No reason to reject the null hypothesis but no particular reason to accept it either. Further sampling required. |

**6. Types of error** There can never be absolute certainty that the correct decision has been made. Despite the fact that the weight of the package differs considerably from the assumed mean, it could, conceivably, have arisen by chance when the machine was functioning properly, and will do so in 1 out of 385 cases. In rejecting the null hypothesis, the decision will on average be incorrect in 1 case out of 385 but correct in the remaining 384 cases. The types of error that could occur are shown below.

| Null hypothesis | Accept hypothesis | Decision Reject hypothesis |
|---|---|---|
| True | Correct decision | Incorrect decision – type I error |
| False | Incorrect decision – type II error | Correct decision |

The lower the significance level, the lower the probability of making a **type I error**. The probability of the type I error in the example is 1 in 385. Assessing the chances of a **type II error** (accepting the null hypothesis when it is false) is very difficult and beyond the scope of this book.

The possibility of error in hypothesis testing is acceptable with a 5% level of significance and underlines the fact *that statistical tests can never prove anything* – all inferences are made with varying degrees of confidence. The alternative, of reducing type I errors by demanding an absurdly low significance level, would lead to all null hypotheses never being rejected, e.g., no evidence would ever convince the production manager that his machine was faulty.

**7. Types of test** At the 5% level, the result of the test outlined above might be as shown in Figure 22.

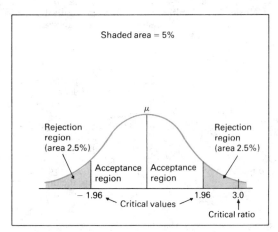

*Figure 22. A two-tail test*

If the critical ratio falls within the **rejection region** (or **critical region**), the *null* hypothesis is rejected and the *alternative* hypothesis is accepted. This decision is reversed when the ratio falls within the **acceptance region**. The diagram illustrates a **two-tail test**, where both tails of the distribution are part of the critical region. **Two-tail tests** are used when values below and above the mean can upset the null hypothesis (formulation (a) on page 68).

Formulation (b) on page 68 tests the hypothesis that the mean has increased. In this case only values well above the mean (but not below it) would provide convincing evidence. **A one-tail test** is appropriate here as shown in Figure 23.

The value of 1.645 has been found from tables by looking up 0.95 (the area of the unshaded region) in the body of the table. Again, this critical ratio lies in the critical region and it is concluded that the machine is producing overweight packages.

This **one-tail test** is appropriate if the production manager had suspicions *before* the package was sampled that the machine was producing overweight packages. Taking first the sample and then deciding the formulation of the hypothesis using the sample values introduces bias to the test and can only lead to totally unreliable conclusions.

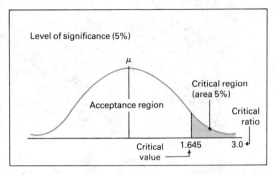

*Figure 23. A one-tail test*

## Distribution of the means of a sample
In practice, a larger size of sample is taken and the mean of the data is used as the sampling statistic.

### Example
A manufacturer claims that the mean breaking point of car safety belts produced in his factory is 2800 pounds. A sample of 100 belts is to be chosen to test his claim.

Therefore, the *null* hypothesis is $\mu = 2800$ (population mean is 2800), while the *alternative* hypothesis is $\mu \neq 2800$.

This is a **two-tail test** because both very low and very high breaking points would be evidence against the claim. The breaking point of belts is a normally distributed variable with mean $\mu = 2800$. The population standard deviation $\sigma$ is not given. An estimate of $\sigma$ can be obtained by finding the standard deviation of the sample values, using the methods illustrated in Chapter 3. In general, this estimate of $\sigma$ will only be reliable for large samples (greater than 50). For smaller samples, a different technique is needed (see page 74). The **sample statistic** is the mean of the sample, $\bar{x}$, and the **sampling distribution** is the distribution of the sample statistic $\bar{x}$. If the breaking points of the seat belts are plotted on a graph, the first normal distribution is obtained as shown in Figure 24. When samples of 100 belts are taken and the mean, $\bar{x}$, of each is plotted, the second normal distribution is produced.

The second curve is thinner than the first because there is less variation in the means (large values in the sample will tend to be cancelled by smaller values). The following result is quoted without proof.

If $x$ is normally distributed with mean $\mu$ and standard deviation $\sigma$, then $\bar{x}$ is normally distributed with mean $\mu$ and standard deviation $\sigma/\sqrt{n}$, where $n$ is the sample size.

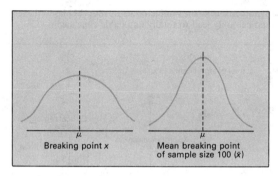

*Figure 24. Safety belt breaking strain*

The standard deviation of the means of a sample is smaller than the standard deviation of single values. For example, when $n$ equals 4, the standard deviation of means is one half of the standard deviation of single values. The ratio $\sigma/\sqrt{n}$ is sometimes called the **standard error of the mean**. Using the same example of 100 seat belts, given a level of significance of $5\%$, the mean of the sample is $\bar{x} = 2769$ pounds and the standard deviation, $s = 200$ pounds. The 100 sample values and the calculations of $\bar{x}$ and $s$ are omitted. In analysis the estimate of $\sigma$ is 200 (from the sample) and the standard error of the mean is $\sigma/\sqrt{n} = 200/\sqrt{100} = 20$.

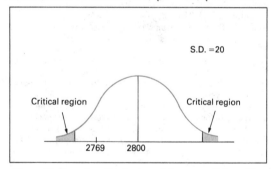

*Figure 25. Sampling distribution of the mean, S.D. = 20*

The critical ratio can be determined with the equation: $z = (\bar{x} - \mu)/(\sigma/\sqrt{n}) = (2769 - 2800)/20 = -1.55$, i.e., the sample mean is 1.55 standard deviations below the expected mean.

The result is not significant at the $5\%$ level (see page 69). There is no evidence to suggest that the manufacturer's claim is false (i.e., the *null* hypothesis is acceptable). The low sample mean of 2769 pounds could have easily arisen from the fluctuations of random sampling.

(*Note* that even if the population is not normally distributed, it can be proven that the distribution of the means of a sample is approximately normally distributed for large sample sizes ($n > 50$). In the present example, the assumption that the breaking points of belts are normally distributed is not absolutely necessary.)

## DIFFERENCE BETWEEN MEANS
## (LARGE SAMPLES)

A manufacturer wishes to test the claim that light bulbs produced by a new process tend to have longer lives than those produced by the standard process. He sampled the bulbs to destruction with the following results.

|  | Sample size | Mean life (h) | S.D. (h) |
|---|---|---|---|
| New process | 60 | 1783 | 113 |
| Old process | 80 | 1721 | 98 |

*Null* hypothesis: there is no difference between the two types of processing.

*Alternative* hypothesis: the new process is better.

A one-tail test is appropriate because the *null* hypothesis would be rejected only if the new process gave significantly better results. Here, the **sample statistics**, or crucial value, is the difference between the two sample means. Under the *null* hypothesis, the difference between the sample means should have an expected mean of zero (see page 70).

The S.E. of the mean of the first sample
$= 113/\sqrt{60} = 14.588$, with variance 212.817.

The S.E. of the mean of the second sample
$= 98/\sqrt{80} = 10.957$, with variance 120.05.

To find the S.E. of the difference between the sample means, the following formula can be used:

Variance of the difference $= $ *Sum* of the two variances (assuming the two samples are independent), i.e.,
Variance of the difference $= 212.817 + 120.05 = 332.867$,
and S.E. of the difference $= \sqrt{332.867} = 18.245$.

The critical ratio is then $\dfrac{1783 - 1721}{18.245} = 3.398$.

Since the critical value for a **one-tail test** at the 5 % level is 1.645 (see page 70), the result is significant – in fact highly significant. The *null* hypothesis is rejected with a high degree of confidence, and the new process produces significantly better results than the old method of production.

## TESTING A PROPORTION

A newspaper claims that it is read by at least 60 % of the town in which it is published. A survey is conducted on a random sample of 1000 residents. Formulate the appropriate decision rule.

*Null* hypothesis: proportion of readers, $p = 0.6$.
*Alternative* hypothesis: $p < 0.6$.

This is a **one-tail test** – the claim would be rejected if the proportion in the sample was too low.

The **sample statistic** is the number of readers in the sample $x$. For the **sampling distribution**, the sample statistic is a discrete variable and has a binomial distribution with parameters of $n = 1000$, $p = 0.6$ and $q = 0.4$. Hence,

Mean $= np = 1000 \times 0.6 = 600$.

S.D. $= \sqrt{npq} = \sqrt{1000 \times 0.6 \times 0.4} = 15.492$.

The normal approximation to the binomial distribution may be applied (see page 63).

Critical ratio $z = (x - 600)/15.492$.

From Figure 23, with the critical region moved to the left, when $z$ is exactly equal to $-1.645$, i.e., when $x = 574.516$, the result is on the border of the critical region.

### Decision rule

| Number of readers in sample | Decision |
|---|---|
| 574 or less | Reject null hypothesis |
| 575 or more | Accept null hypothesis |

*Note* The actual proportion of readers in the sample could have been chosen as the sample statistic, with the following change.

Mean of a proportion $= p$.

S.E. of a proportion $= \sqrt{\dfrac{pq}{n}}$.

(This would of course give the same decision rule.)

## THE $t$-DISTRIBUTION

All the problems investigated so far in this chapter have used large sample sizes. This can be costly in practice and tests have been developed to deal with smaller samples (size $< 50$).

## Example

The production at a chemical plant should be 100 lb. per hour. Observations of the output during each hour of the day produced the following outputs: 93, 97, 101, 95, 98, 95, 99, 98. Is the production rate significantly different from what might be expected?

The sample size is $n = 8$ and the standard deviation of this sample cannot be employed as a reliable estimate of the S.D. of the population because the sample is too small. In other words, the normal distribution test of a sample mean must not be applied in this case. Another distribution, called **the t-distribution**, allows for this unreliability. It is shown in Figure 26, together with the normal distribution, for purposes of comparison.

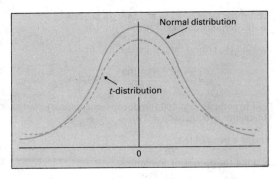

*Figure 26. t-curve and normal distribution*

The t-curve is thinner and has longer tails than the normal distribution curve. For each sample size, a slightly different t-distribution is produced. The one illustrated in Figure 26 has $v = 7$ **degrees of freedom** and is applicable to samples of size eight. The test can be made according to the following steps.

**1.** Calculate the sample mean $\bar{x}$:

$$\bar{x} = (93 + 97 + 101 + 95 + 98 + 95 + 99 + 98)/8 = 97.$$

**2.** Calculate the sample S.D., using the formula:

$$s = \sqrt{\frac{1}{n-1}\Sigma(x - \bar{x})^2}.$$

The sum of the squared deviations is divided by $n-1$ and not $n$. This tends to give a better estimate of the population S.D., despite it still being a poor estimate for small samples.

| $x$ | $x - \bar{x}$ | $(x - \bar{x})^2$ |
|-----|------|-------|
| 93  | -4   | 16    |
| 97  | 0    | 0     |
| 101 | 4    | 16    |
| 95  | -2   | 4     |
| 98  | 1    | 1     |
| 95  | -2   | 4     |
| 99  | 2    | 4     |
| 98  | 1    | 1     |
|     |      | 46    |

Therefore, $n = 8$ and $s = \sqrt{\dfrac{46}{7}}$

$$= 2.563.$$

**3**. Determine the S.E. of the sample mean.

S.E. of the mean $= s/\sqrt{n} = 2.563/\sqrt{8} = 0.906$
(cf. the formula on page 72).

**4**. Find the critical ratio (now denoted by $t$).

$$t = \frac{\bar{x} - \mu}{s/\sqrt{n}} = \frac{97 - 100}{0.906} = -3.311.$$

*Null* hypothesis: $\mu = 100$ (production rate normal).
*Alternative* hypothesis: $\mu \neq 100$.

This is a two-tail test.

**5**. Find the degrees of freedom, $v$.

$$v = n - 1 = 8 - 1 = 7.$$

**6**. From the $t$-tables in the Appendix the critical value for seven degrees of freedom at the 5% level is 2.37.
The $t$-distribution for $v = 7$ is shown in Figure 27.

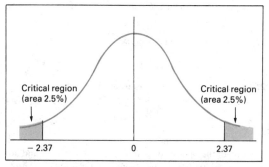

*Figure 27. t-distribution ($v = 7$)*

Since the observed value of $t$, $-3.311$, lies in the critical region, the result is significant at the 5% level. The production rate cannot reasonably be attributed to natural variations.

In general, the $t$-test requires larger critical values than the normal distribution tests, a consequence of the population's S.D. not being known with any degree of reliability. As the sample size increases, the $t$-curve approaches the normal curve.

*Note* The $t$-test can only be applied to populations which are normally distributed, or nearly so.

## PAIRED SAMPLES

Ten pairs of disc brake pads were tested, one of each pair having been impregnated with a new type of resin. The wear (in '000s) was measured for each pad, with the following results:

| Pair no. | 1 | 2 | 3 | 4 | 5 | 6 | 7 | 8 | 9 | 10 |
|---|---|---|---|---|---|---|---|---|---|---|
| Control pad | 95.1 | 89.2 | 91.5 | 99.3 | 100.8 | 81.6 | 90.0 | 85.4 | 94.6 | 92.6 |
| Impregnated pad | 93.2 | 96.5 | 87.2 | 99.2 | 96.3 | 85.4 | 84.7 | 84.2 | 90.3 | 95.1 |

Does the new resin affect the wear rate?

A $t$-test is appropriate because of the small sample size. Only the difference between the wear of each pair of pads is relevant.

| Pair no. | 1 | 2 | 3 | 4 | 5 | 6 | 7 | 8 | 9 | 10 |
|---|---|---|---|---|---|---|---|---|---|---|
| Difference in wear | 1.9 | −7.3 | 4.3 | 0.1 | 4.5 | −3.8 | 5.3 | 1.2 | 4.3 | −2.5 |

The calculations can now be performed on this table in exactly the same manner as the example given in the last section.

*Null* hypothesis: $\mu = 0$ (no difference).
*Alternative* hypothesis: $\mu \neq 0$ (two-tail test).

Sample size, $n = 10$.

Sample mean, $\bar{x} = 8/10 = 0.8$.
Sample S.D., $s = \sqrt{157.96/9} = 4.189$ using the formula on page 75.
S.E. of sample mean, $s/\sqrt{n} = 4.189/\sqrt{10} = 1.325$.

Critical ratio, $t = \dfrac{\bar{x} - \mu}{s/\sqrt{n}} = \dfrac{0.8 - 0}{1.325} = 0.604$.

Degrees of freedom, $v = n - 1 = 9$.

The critical value is 2.26 at the 5% level (from tables, at nine degrees of freedom).

The result is not significant at the 5% level because the critical ratio is numerically less than the critical value. There is no evidence that the new resin affects the wear rate.

## Difference between means (small samples)

For samples which are unpaired, the t-test of the difference between sample means is a little more complicated.

## Example

Prospective employees of a company took an intelligence test with the following results.

| Background | No. in sample | Mean score | Standard deviation |
|---|---|---|---|
| Computers | $n_1 = 14$ | $\bar{x}_1 = 75.3$ | $s_1 = 10.61$ |
| Science | $n_2 = 16$ | $\bar{x}_2 = 70.2$ | $s_2 = 12.42$ |

(The standard deviations have been calculated using a divisor of $n-1$.) Is the difference between the means significant?

*Null* hypothesis: $\mu = 0$ (the two populations are the same).
*Alternative* hypothesis: $\mu \neq 0$.

To find $s$ – the best estimate possible of the population's S.D. – the following formula is used.

$$s^2 = \frac{(n_1 - 1)s_1^2 + (n_2 - 1)s_2^2}{n_1 + n_2 - 2}$$

i.e., $s^2 = \dfrac{13 \times 10.61^2 + 15 \times 12.42^2}{14 + 16 - 2} = 134.903$

$$s = \sqrt{134.903} = \underline{11.615}$$

S.E. of means of the first sample = $s/\sqrt{n_1} = 11.615/\sqrt{14}$ = 3.104, with variance 9.636.

S.E. of means of the second sample = $s/\sqrt{n_2} = 11.615/\sqrt{16}$ = 2.904, with variance 8.431.

Variance of the difference between the two means = the *sum* of the two variances (assuming the samples are independent) = 9.636 + 8.431 = 18.067.
Therefore, the S.E. of the difference = $\sqrt{18.067} = 4.251$.

Critical ratio, $t = \dfrac{\bar{x}_1 - \bar{x}_2}{\text{S.E. of difference}} = \dfrac{75.3 - 70.2}{4.251} = 1.2$.

Degrees of freedom, $v = n_1 + n_2 - 2 = 14 + 16 - 2 = 28$.

Critical value at 5% level = 2.05 (see Appendix).

The result is therefore not significant – there is no evidence to suggest that the two types of candidates perform any differently in the test.

*Note* There is a slight difference of approach between a *t*-test and a normal test of the difference between two means.

## ESTIMATION

A market research organization wishes to estimate the number of households currently using a certain product. A random sample of 100 households is taken and, of these, 32 use the product.

The problem here is to estimate an unknown **population parameter** $p$ (proportion of all households using the product) given the value of a **sample statistic** $P = 0.32$ (the proportion in the sample using the product).

The best single estimate of $p$ is clearly 0.32 but the reliability of this figure will depend on the sample size. A sample as small as five, for example, would not be regarded as being sufficiently large to give a reasonable estimate. In practice, it is better to quote a range of values within which $p$ is likely to lie. From page 75, it can be seen that the distribution of the sample proportion $P$ is approximately normal.

One possible approach to the problem is to set up all possible null hypotheses and find the range of values of $p$ which give non-significant results at the 5 % level, e.g.,

*Null* hypothesis: $p = 0.4$

Alternative hypothesis: $p \neq 4$.

S.E. of proportion $= \sqrt{\dfrac{pq}{n}} = \sqrt{\dfrac{0.4 \times 0.6}{100}} = 0.049$.

Critical ratio, $z = \dfrac{0.32 - 0.4}{\text{S.E.}} = \dfrac{-0.08}{0.049} = -1.63$.

This result is not significant at the 5 % level.

Similarly, by trial and error:

$p = 0.41$ gives a non-significant result.
$p = 0.42$ gives a significant result.
$p = 0.23$ gives a significant result.
$p = 0.24$ gives a non-significant result.

The range of values of $p$ in which the null hypothesis is not rejected is approximately 0.24 to 0.41. This is called the **95 % confidence interval** of the population proportion $p$, i.e., the value of $p$ lies between these limits, with probability at 95 %. Again, it is impossible to be certain that $p$ lies within its **confidence limits** and the best that can be achieved is a high degree of confidence.

In this example, the sample is too small to give a reliable estimate of $p$ because any value from 0.24 to 0.41 could reasonably explain the sample proportion of 0.32. To speed up the calculation of confidence intervals, the following formula can be used for normal distributions.

The 95% confidence limits of a population parameter are the corresponding sample statistic value $\pm 1.96 \times$ S.E. of the statistic. In this example, the formula produces:

$$0.32 \pm 1.96 \times \sqrt{pq/100}.$$

Unfortunately, the population parameter $p$ appears in this formula. An approximation can still be obtained by replacing $p$ by the sample proportion, 0.32, as shown below:

$$\text{Limits:} \ = 0.32 \pm 1.96 \times \sqrt{\frac{0.32 \times 0.68}{100}}$$

$$= 0.32 \pm 0.09 \text{ to two decimal places.}$$

i.e.,         $0.32 - 0.09$ to $0.32 + 0.09$ (i.e., 0.23 to 0.41).

These are nearly the same values as the more accurate version gave but the method of evaluation is much easier.

### Example
A sample of eight items produced by a machine has a mean weight, $\bar{x}$, of 5 lb. and a standard deviation, $s$, of 0.1 lb. Find the confidence limits for the mean weight of the population.

This is a small sample, so the $t$-distribution applies.

S.E. of the sample mean $= s/\sqrt{n} = 0.1/\sqrt{8} = 0.0354$.
Degrees of freedom, $v = n - 1 = 8 - 1 = 7$.
5% point of the $t$-distribution, $(v = 7) = 2.37$.
The formula above can be used but the value of 1.96 is replaced by 2.37.
95% confidence limits for the population mean are:

$5 \pm 2.37 \times 0.0354$, i.e., 4.92 to 5.08, to two decimal places.

If the nominal weight of the items is outside this range, the machine is probably malfunctioning.

### SAMPLE SIZE

Polling organizations do not choose just any sample size for their research. A sample which is too small undermines the reliability of an estimate and a sample which is too large may be far too costly or time wasting. The size of a sample can be determined once the accuracy required is chosen. For example, a poll to determine the proportion $p$ in the example on estimation (see page 79) might have to achieve a single estimate within 0.01 of the true answer (with 95% confidence). The minimum sample size required to do this is calculated as follows.

Range of a 95 % confidence interval $= 2 \times 1.96 \times$ S.E. for a normally distributed statistic.

Required range $= 2 \times 0.01 = 0.02$ (from the stated accuracy to be achieved). Hence, $0.02 = 2 \times 1.96 \times \sqrt{pq/n}$.

The unknown $p$ appears again in this equation and the sample to estimate it has not been taken at this stage. This problem can be overcome by undertaking a preliminary survey on a reasonably sized sample or by using past data to estimate $p$ from the sample proportion. These methods can be open to criticism and a sounder approach uses the value of $p$ which gives the largest sample size. This occurs when $p = 0.5$ and $q = 0.5$ because the values are the same and are therefore harder to estimate accurately.

Hence, $0.02 = 2 \times 1.96 \times 0.5/\sqrt{n}$

i.e., $0.02 = 3.92 \times 0.5/\sqrt{n}$;

$0.02 = 1.96/\sqrt{n}$; $\sqrt{n} = 1.96/0.02 = 98$.

Where $n = 9604$

A sample of size 9604 is needed to be 95 % confident of the sample proportion being within 0.01 of the population proportion. Other sample sizes are shown in the following table.

| Desired accuracy | Sample size needed |
|---|---|
| Within 0.005 | 38 416 |
| Within 0.01 | 9 604 |
| Within 0.02 | 2 401 |
| Within 0.05 | 384 |
| Within 0.1 | 96 |

In other words, to double the accuracy requires four times the sample size. It can be very costly to achieve a high degree of accuracy, therefore. Sample sizes can be calculated in a similar fashion for means of samples, using the normal or $t$-distribution when applicable.

The above calculations for determining the sample size apply only to simple, random sampling when questionnaire design factors do not have to be taken into account.

# Chapter 6

# Associative Data Analysis

## CORRELATION

Correlation is an indication of the degree of *association* between two variables or, more accurately, the amount of reduction in error in predicting values of one variable from values of the other. In particular, **the product moment correlation coefficient**, $r$ (or simply **the correlation coefficient**), measures the degree of *linear* association between two variables. If, for example, the prices of a product over the last few years are plotted against the demand during those years, some of the possible graphical representations that might be obtained are shown in Figure 28.

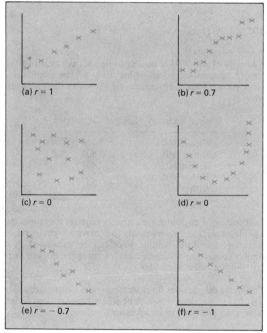

*Figure 28. Scatter diagrams*

Typical values of the correlation coefficient are shown below each **scatter diagram**. Graphs (a) and (f) illustrate perfect linear relationships, (b) and (e) close linear relationships and (c) no relationship. In graph (d) a perfect parabolic relationship is shown but the value of $r$ is zero because of the lack of any linearity.

The correlation coefficient $r$ always takes values in the range $-1$ to $+1$.

When $r$ is positive, the variables tend to increase together or decrease together, i.e., they are **directly or positively correlated**.

When $r$ is negative, as one variable increases (decreases) the other tends to decrease (increase), i.e., the variables are **indirectly or negatively correlated**.

For large absolute values of $r$ (close to $+1$ or $-1$), predictions of future demand, for example, can be made with confidence, but low values of $r$ make predictions practically worthless. In the case of zero correlation, the variables are said to be **uncorrelated** – no linear relationship exists.

A value of $r = 0.5$ does not mean double the association of $r = 0.25$, nor is an increase from 0.4 to 0.6 equivalent to one from 0.7 to 0.9. The correlation coefficient is an *index number*, not a measurement on a linear scale. However, a value of $-0.6$ indicates just as close a relationship as one of $+0.6$.

## EVALUATION OF $r$

The calculation of the correlation coefficient is illustrated in the table below for the prices and demands given in the first two columns.

| Price $x$ ($) | Demand $y$ ('000s) | $x-\bar{x}$ | $y-\bar{y}$ | $(x-\bar{x})^2$ | $(y-\bar{y})^2$ | $(x-\bar{x})(y-\bar{y})$ |
|---|---|---|---|---|---|---|
| 27 | 18 | $-9$ | 5 | 81 | 25 | $-45$ |
| 29 | 16 | $-7$ | 3 | 49 | 9 | $-21$ |
| 32 | 15 | $-4$ | 2 | 16 | 4 | $-8$ |
| 36 | 12 | 0 | $-1$ | 0 | 1 | 0 |
| 37 | 12 | 1 | $-1$ | 1 | 1 | $-1$ |
| 40 | 11 | 4 | $-2$ | 16 | 4 | $-8$ |
| 42 | 10 | 6 | $-3$ | 36 | 9 | $-18$ |
| 45 | 10 | 9 | $-3$ | 81 | 9 | $-27$ |
| 288 | 104 | | | 280 | 62 | $-128$ |

**1.** The number of paired values $n = 8$.

**2.** The mean price $\bar{x} = \dfrac{288}{8} = 36$.

**3.** The mean demand $\bar{y} = \dfrac{104}{8} = 13$.

**4.** The deviations from the means are shown in the third and fourth columns.

**5.** The squared deviations and the product of the deviations are shown in the remaining columns with the totals.

**6.** The standard deviation of the prices, $s_x$, is

$$s_x = \sqrt{\frac{1}{n}\Sigma(x-\bar{x})^2} = \sqrt{\frac{280}{8}} = 5.916.$$

**7.** The standard deviation of the demands, $s_y$, is

$$s_y = \sqrt{\frac{1}{n}\Sigma(y-\bar{y})^2} = \sqrt{\frac{62}{8}} = 2.784.$$

**8.** The **covariance** of $x$ and $y$, written $s_{xy}$, is

$$s_{xy} = \frac{1}{n}\Sigma(x-\bar{x})(y-\bar{y}) = \frac{-128}{8} = -16.$$

**9.** The correlation coefficient, $r$, is

$$r = \frac{s_{xy}}{s_x s_y} = \frac{-16}{5.916 \times 2.784} = -0.97 \text{ to two decimal places.}$$

This value of $r$ is very close to $-1$ and indicates that the variables are highly indirectly correlated. The significance of this value can be tested to see whether it could have occurred by chance, owing to the small sample size (see page 85). At step **9** above, the covariance is divided by the product of the two standard deviations to ensure that $r$ is *dimensionless*, i.e., $r$ has no units unlike the mean and standard deviation. The covariance itself is a raw measure of linear association and is increased by two positive or two negative deviations, and decreased by two deviations of differing signs.

## ALTERNATIVE FORMULAE

There are other equivalent forms of the formula for $r$ which are sometimes easier to apply, e.g.,

$$r = \frac{\Sigma(x-\bar{x})(y-\bar{y})}{\sqrt{\Sigma(x-\bar{x})^2\Sigma(y-\bar{y})^2}}$$

Note that this formula is equivalent to the one shown in No. 9 above since $n$ is the numerator and denominator cancels out.

If the means are not whole numbers, the above formula becomes a little harder to use. An alternative version is:

$$r = \frac{\Sigma xy - n\bar{x}\bar{y}}{\sqrt{(\Sigma x^2 - n\bar{x}^2)(\Sigma y^2 - n\bar{y}^2)}}$$

**Example**

| Price index A | Price index B | $x$ | $y$ | $x^2$ | $y^2$ | $xy$ |
|---|---|---|---|---|---|---|
| 98 | 101 | 10 | 6 | 100 | 36 | 60 |
| 96 | 102 | 8 | 7 | 64 | 49 | 56 |
| 88 | 100 | 0 | 5 | 0 | 25 | 0 |
| 84 | 98 | -4 | 3 | 16 | 9 | -12 |
| 84 | 94 | -4 | -1 | 16 | 1 | 4 |
| 80 | 95 | -8 | 0 | 64 | 0 | 0 |
| 83 | 92 | -5 | -3 | 25 | 9 | 15 |
| 87 | 91 | -1 | -4 | 1 | 16 | 4 |
| 93 | 94 | 5 | -1 | 25 | 1 | -5 |
| 96 | 95 | 8 | 0 | 64 | 0 | 0 |
| | | 9 | 12 | 375 | 146 | 122 |

**1.** The data can be coded (see page 38) to make the calculations even easier. *Coding does not affect the value of r.* Price index *A* has been coded by subtracting 88 from it and price index *B* has been reduced by 95. This is shown in the next two columns. The actual indices are not needed again in the calculation.

**2.** $\bar{x} = \dfrac{9}{10} = 0.9, \quad \bar{y} = \dfrac{12}{10} = 1.2.$

The second formula on page 84 will be applied because the means are not whole numbers.

**3.** The last three columns are evaluated – deviations from the mean are not needed.

**4.** $r = \dfrac{122 - 10 \times 0.9 \times 1.2}{\sqrt{(375 - 10 \times 0.9^2)(146 - 10 \times 1.2^2)}} = 0.51.$

($n = 10$ because there are 10 paired values in the table.)

## RELIABILITY OF *r*

A small sample may give a high correlation coefficient purely by chance. To test the significance of *r*, the following procedure is applied (assuming the variables are normally distributed).

**1.** Null hypothesis: The variables are uncorrelated.

**2.** Alternative hypothesis: There is some degree of linear association between the variables (two-tail test).

**3.** Calculate $X = 0.5 \ln \dfrac{1+r}{1-r}.$ (ln means the logarithm to base e.)

Then *X* is approximately normally distributed with mean 0 and standard deviation

$$\frac{1}{\sqrt{n-3}}.$$

For example, from page 83, $n = 8$ and $r = -0.97$.

$X = 0.5 \ln \dfrac{1-0.97}{1+0.97} = -2.092,$ mean 0, S.D. $= \dfrac{1}{\sqrt{8-3}}$

$= 0.447.$

Critical ratio $z = \dfrac{-2.092}{0.447} = -4.68.$

This result is significant at the 5 % level.

The evidence suggests that the variables are correlated.

For example, from page 85, $n = 10$ and $r = 0.51$.

$$X = 0.5 \ln \frac{1+0.51}{1-0.51} = 0.563, \text{ mean } 0, \text{ S.D.} = \frac{1}{\sqrt{10-3}}$$

$$= 0.378.$$

Critical ratio $z = \dfrac{0.563}{0.378} = 1.49$.

This result is not significant at the 5% level. There is no evidence to suggest that the variables are correlated – the value of $r$ is consistent with the random fluctuations of uncorrelated variables. Predictions of Index $B$ from Index $A$ (or vice versa) are not reliable.

In general, the larger the sample size, the smaller $r$ has to be to give a significant result. This means that smaller samples are more likely to give **spurious correlations**.

For example, if $n = 100$ and $r = 0.2$.

$$X = 0.5 \ln \frac{1+0.2}{1-0.2} = 0.203, \text{ mean } 0, \text{ S.D.} = \frac{1}{\sqrt{100-3}}$$

$$= 0.102.$$

Critical ratio $z = \dfrac{0.203}{0.102} = 2.00$.

This is significant at the 5% level. The variables are correlated but the degree of association is small.


## INTERPRETATION OF $r$

A high correlation coefficient indicates some causal connection or some common factor(s) between the variables, but extreme care must be taken when interpreting such a connection. For example, there is a high correlation coefficient between the size of shoe and handwriting speed of children of various ages. This does not mean that by improving a child's writing speed his feet will grow longer. The simple common factor in this example is age – as a child grows older both his shoe size and his writing speed tend to increase.

Two variables which are both increasing or both decreasing from year to year may have a significant coefficient of correlation. If the two variables are totally unrelated the reason for the correlation is the general upward or downward trend of both factors. Such a correlation is called a **spurious correlation**. A correlation is a measure of association, not a measure of cause and effect. Nevertheless, the coefficient can be a useful tool in statistical analysis when used sensibly.

## RANK CORRELATION

When a measure of association is required for *qualitative* factors such as taste preference or depth of color, the method of ranking can be applied. Two duplicate tests are given to a food-taster on different days. On each occasion he ranks nine brands of a food product.

| Brand | Rank (first test) | Rank (second test) | $d$ | $d^2$ |
|-------|-------------------|--------------------|-----|-------|
| A | 3 | 2 | 1 | 1 |
| B | 7 | 8 | −1 | 1 |
| C | 4 | 6 | −2 | 4 |
| D | 1 | 1 | 0 | 0 |
| E | 6 | 4 | 2 | 4 |
| F | 9 | 7 | 2 | 4 |
| G | 2 | 3 | −1 | 1 |
| H | 8 | 9 | −1 | 1 |
| I | 5 | 5 | 0 | 0 |
| | | | | 16 |

**Spearman's coefficient of rank correlation** $R$ is the product moment correlation coefficient between the two sets of ranks. It can be evaluated using the simpler formula:

$$R = 1 - \frac{6\Sigma d^2}{n^3 - n}$$

where $n$ is the number of paired ranks and $d$ is the difference between the ranks.

In this example, $n = 9$, and the evaluation of the sum of the squared differences in the ranks is shown in the table above.

Then $R = 1 - \dfrac{6 \times 16}{9^3 - 9} = 1 - \dfrac{96}{720} = 0.87$ to two decimal places.

$R$ gives a measure of the *reliability* of the food-taster in this example. If the two sets of ranks were made by different judges, $R$ would measure the *degree of agreement* between them. The significance test on page 85 is not strictly applicable to $R$, although it can be used as a rough guide.

Again, $R$ lies between $-1$ and $+1$ with the following interpretations:

| | |
|---|---|
| $R = +1$ | Perfect agreement. |
| $R = 0.5$ | Some degree of agreement. |
| $R = 0$ | Neither agreement nor disagreement. |
| $R = -0.5$ | Some degree of disagreement. |
| $R = -1$ | Perfect disagreement. |

If some of the ranks are tied, the above formula gives a good approximation to the correlation coefficient, as long as there are not too many ties.

## LINEAR REGRESSION

This technique determines the **line of best fit** of a set of data. The graph below shows the scatter diagram for the sales of a product during the past ten years.

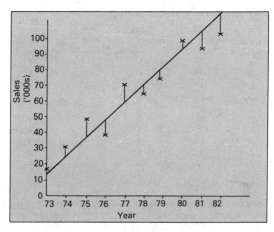

*Figure 29. Sales of a product*

The line of best fit has been drawn freehand. The vertical lines are the deviations of the observations from this line. The quantitative technique of finding the equation of the **regression line** (line of best fit) uses the **least squares method**, i.e., the sum of the squares of the deviations is made as small as possible. The mathematical derivation of the formula is omitted.

The year in this example is called the **independent variable** and the sales figure is the **dependent variable**. Regression analysis predicts values of the *dependent variable* given values of the *independent variable*. The calculations proceed as follows.

| $x$(year) | $y$(sales) | $x^2$ | $y^2$ | $xy$ |
|---|---|---|---|---|
| 0 | 17 | 0 | 289 | 0 |
| 1 | 32 | 1 | 1024 | 32 |
| 2 | 48 | 4 | 2304 | 96 |
| 3 | 39 | 9 | 1521 | 117 |
| 4 | 70 | 16 | 4900 | 280 |
| 5 | 63 | 25 | 3969 | 315 |
| 6 | 72 | 36 | 5184 | 432 |
| 7 | 98 | 49 | 9604 | 686 |
| 8 | 96 | 64 | 9216 | 768 |
| 9 | 100 | 81 | 10 000 | 900 |
| 45 | 635 | 285 | 48 011 | 3626 |

**1.** The year $x$ has been coded to simplify the calculations – year 0 means 1973. Then,

$$\bar{x} = \frac{45}{10} = 4.5 \quad \bar{y} = \frac{635}{10} = 63.5.$$

**2.** S.D. of $x$, $\quad s_x = \sqrt{\frac{1}{n}(\Sigma x^2 - n\bar{x}^2)} = \sqrt{\frac{1}{10}(285 - 10 \times 4.5^2)}$

$$= 2.872.$$

S.D. of $y$, $\quad s_y = \sqrt{\frac{1}{n}(\Sigma y^2 - n\bar{y}^2)}$

$$= \sqrt{\frac{1}{10}(48\,011 - 10 \times 63.5^2)} = 27.728.$$

Covariance, $s_{xy} = \frac{1}{n}(\Sigma xy - n\bar{x}\bar{y})$

$$= \frac{1}{10}(3626 - 10 \times 4.5 \times 63.5) = 76.85.$$

These formulae are the alternative versions, which do not use deviations from the mean. The standard deviation of $y$ is not needed for the regression line but the correlation coefficient will be calculated to give a measure of the predictive ability of the line.

**3.** $r = \dfrac{s_{xy}}{s_x s_y} = \dfrac{76.85}{2.872 \times 27.728} = 0.965.$

The **regression coefficient**

$$b = \frac{s_{xy}}{s_x^2} = \frac{76.85}{2.872^2} = 9.32.$$

The **regression constant**

$$a = \bar{y} - b\bar{x} = 63.5 - 9.32 \times 4.5 = 21.56.$$

(The factor of $1/n$ in the three formulae of step **2** may be omitted if desired.)

**4.** The equation of the regression line is given by:
$y = bx + a$, i.e., sales $y = 9.32x + 21.56$ where $x$ is the year.

**5.** Predicted sales in 1983, i.e., Year 10, are:
$y = 9.32 \times 10 + 21.56 = 114.76$, from the above equation.
Predicted sales in 1984, i.e., Year 11 are:
$y = 9.32 \times 11 + 21.56 = 124.08$ ('000s).

**6.** The significant test of $r$ on page 85 should not be applied because the time variable $x$ is certainly *not* normally distributed. However, the square of the correlation coefficient, sometimes called the **coefficient of determination**, gives a measure of the amount of variation in the sales figures which has been explained by the regression line.

The coefficient of determination is given by $r^2 = 0.965^2 = 0.93$, i.e., 93 %. Thus, only 7 % of the variation in the sales figures is not attributable to the time factor.

**Regression analysis** is suitable for long-term forecasting as long as there are no new influences that might upset the general trend. The further the projection is made into the future, the more uncertain the estimates become.

### Example
Perform a time series analysis on the following data, fitting the trend using algebraic methods.

| Year | Quarter | $x$ | Sales ($y$) | Trend | TF | SV | RF |
|------|---------|-----|-------------|-------|------|--------|-------|
| 1980 | 1 | 0 | 53 | 41.85 | +11.15 | +7.55 | +3.60 |
| 1980 | 2 | 1 | 31 | 43.33 | −12.33 | −17.59 | +5.26 |
| 1980 | 3 | 2 | 40 | 44.81 | −4.81 | −6.74 | +1.93 |
| 1980 | 4 | 3 | 61 | 46.29 | +14.71 | +16.78 | −2.07 |
| 1981 | 1 | 4 | 55 | 47.78 | +7.22 | +7.55 | −0.33 |
| 1981 | 2 | 5 | 32 | 49.26 | −17.26 | −17.59 | +0.33 |
| 1981 | 3 | 6 | 43 | 50.74 | −7.74 | −6.74 | −1.00 |
| 1981 | 4 | 7 | 67 | 52.22 | +14.78 | +16.78 | −2.00 |
| 1982 | 1 | 8 | 58 | 53.71 | +4.29 | +7.55 | −3.26 |
| 1982 | 2 | 9 | 32 | 55.19 | −23.19 | −17.59 | −5.60 |
| 1982 | 3 | 10 | 49 | 56.67 | −7.67 | −6.74 | −0.93 |
| 1982 | 4 | 11 | 79 | 58.15 | +20.85 | +16.78 | +4.07 |

The $x$ column gives the number of the period.
Total number of observations $n = 12$.

$$\bar{x} = 5.5, \quad \bar{y} = 50, \quad \Sigma x^2 = 506, \quad \Sigma xy = 3512.$$

Regression coefficient, $b = \dfrac{3512 - 12 \times 5.5 \times 50}{506 - 12 \times 5.5 \times 5.5} = 1.4825.$

Regression constant, $a = 50 - 1.4825 \times 5.5 = 41.8462.$

Regression line is $y = 1.4825x + 41.8462.$

The trend is shown in the fifth column, the values being calculated from the above equation.

The fluctuations from the trend (TF) are evaluated by subtracting the trend from the actual sales in each period. The seasonal totals are given below.

| Quarter | Fluctuations | | | Totals | Average |
|---------|------|------|------|--------|---------|
| 1 | +11.15, | +7.22, | +4.29 | +22.66 | +7.55 |
| 2 | −12.33, | −17.26, | −23.19 | −52.78 | −17.59 |
| 3 | −4.81, | −7.74, | −7.67 | −20.22 | −6.74 |
| 4 | +14.71, | +14.78, | +20.85 | +50.34 | +16.78 |

The **seasonal variation** (SV) is shown in the table.

The **residual fluctuation** (RF) is the trend fluctuation minus the seasonal variation and represents the variation unaccounted for in this analysis. The table below gives 1983 predictions.

| Quarter | Trend (regression line) | SV | Prediction |
|---------|------------------------|--------|------------|
| 1 | 59.64 ($x = 12$) | =7.55 | 67.19 |
| 2 | 61.12 ($x = 13$) | −17.59 | 43.53 |
| 3 | 62.60 ($x = 14$) | −6.74 | 55.86 |
| 4 | 64.08 ($x = 15$) | +16.78 | 80.86 |

## CURVILINEAR REGRESSION

If the points plotted on a scatter diagram obviously do not suggest a linear relationship, it is possible to fit other curves to the data. The only type of curve considered is that of the **exponential function**. General **curvilinear regression** and **multilinear regression** (more than two variables) are beyond the scope of this book.

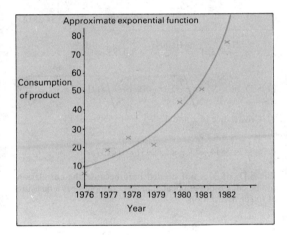

*Figure 30. Consumption of a product*

The scatter diagram in Figure 30 illustrates approximate **exponential growth**, i.e., the consumption increases by roughly the same proportion each year.

The exponential function has the general formula:

$$y = ab^x$$

where $y$ is the consumption (dependent variable), $x$ the year (independent variable) and $a$ and $b$ are parameters to be determined by the regression analysis.

The above equation can be reduced to linear form by taking the logarithm of both sides:

$$\log y = \log a + x \log b.$$

This equation will be rewritten as:

$$Y + A + bx \quad \text{where} \quad Y = \log y, \ A = \log a, \ B = \log b.$$

The method of the last section can now be repeated using $Y$, $A$ and $B$ in place of $y$, $a$ and $b$ respectively.

Coded year Consumption

| $x$ | $y$ | $Y = \log y$ | $x^2$ | $xY$ |
|---|---|---|---|---|
| 0 | 6 | 0.7782 | 0 | 0 |
| 1 | 19 | 1.2788 | 1 | 1.2788 |
| 2 | 25 | 1.3979 | 4 | 2.7958 |
| 3 | 22 | 1.3424 | 9 | 4.0272 |
| 4 | 43 | 1.6335 | 16 | 6.5340 |
| 5 | 50 | 1.6990 | 25 | 8.4950 |
| 6 | 75 | 1.8751 | 36 | 11.2506 |
| 21 | | 10.0049 | 91 | 34.3814 |

**1.** $\bar{x} = \dfrac{21}{7} = 3, \ Y = \dfrac{10.0049}{7} = 1.4293.$

**2.** S.D. of $x$, $S_x = \sqrt{\dfrac{1}{7}(\Sigma x^2 - n\bar{x}^2)} = \sqrt{\dfrac{1}{7}(91 - 7 \times 3^2)} = 2.$

Covariance of $x$ and $Y$, $S_{xy} = \dfrac{1}{n}(\Sigma xY - n\bar{x}Y)$

$= \dfrac{1}{7}(34.3814 - 7 \times 3 \times 1.4293) = 0.6237.$

The S.D. of $Y$ is not needed here because the correlation coefficient $r$ is not applicable in this example – $r$ is a measure of *linear* association.

**3.** Regression coefficient $B = \dfrac{S_{xy}}{S_x^2} = \dfrac{0.6237}{2^2} = 0.1559.$

Regression constant
$A = \bar{Y} - B\bar{x} = 1.4293 - 0.1559 \times 3 = 0.9616.$

**4.** The constants $A$ and $B$ for the linear form of the equation are now converted to those of the exponential equation.

$B = 0.1559$, i.e., $\log b = 0.1559$, i.e., $b = 10^{0.1559} = 1.4319.$

$A = 0.9616$, i.e., $\log a = 0.9616$, i.e., $a = 10^{0.9616} = 9.1538.$

The exponential equation is $y = 9.1538 \times 1.4319^x.$

**5.** Using this equation, the observed and predicted values of the consumption can be compared.

| Year | $x$ | Observed consumption | Predicted consumption |
|------|-----|---------------------|----------------------|
| 1976 | 0 | 6 | 9.1538 |
| 1977 | 1 | 19 | 13.1073 |
| 1978 | 2 | 25 | 18.7684 |
| 1979 | 3 | 22 | 26.8744 |
| 1980 | 4 | 43 | 38.4815 |
| 1981 | 5 | 50 | 55.1017 |
| 1982 | 6 | 75 | 78.9001 |
| 1983 | 7 |  | 112.9771 |
| 1984 | 8 |  | 161.7718 |

This technique can also be applied to exponential *decay*, when the observations *decrease* by the same proportion each year.

## EXPONENTIAL SMOOTHING

This forecasting technique is very easy to apply and is reliable for *short-term predictions*. It uses a weighted moving average, the older observations receiving less weight than more recent observations. In general, regression analysis applies to data with a definite upward or downward trend, but this method can cope well with more periodic data. It is based on the formula:

New forecast = $\alpha \times$ Latest observation $+ (1 - \alpha) \times$ Old forecast.

$\alpha$ is called the **smoothing constant** and takes a value between zero and one, though values in the range 0.1 to 0.3 are usual in practice. If $\alpha$ has a high value, more weight is given to the latest observation and the forecasts tend to reflect the changing observations. If $\alpha$ is small, more weight is given to the old forecast and the forecasts tend to reflect any trend (equivalent to using a long period for a moving average). A value of 0.2 for the smoothing constant means, in effect, that 20% of the fluctuations are real changes in the observations and the remaining 80% are random. The technique is illustrated below for a value of 0.2 for $\alpha$.

| Year | Old forecast | Latest observation | New forecast | Actual sales | Error |
|------|-------------|-------------------|--------------|--------------|-------|
| 1974 | – | – | – | 35 | – |
| 1975 | – | 35 | 35.00 | 34 | +1.00 |
| 1976 | 35.00 | 34 | 34.80 | 36 | −1.20 |
| 1977 | 34.80 | 36 | 35.04 | 31 | +4.04 |
| 1978 | 35.04 | 31 | 34.23 | 28 | +6.23 |
| 1979 | 34.23 | 28 | 32.99 | 30 | +2.99 |
| 1980 | 32.99 | 30 | 32.39 | 27 | +5.39 |
| 1981 | 32.39 | 27 | 31.31 | 26 | +5.31 |
| 1982 | 31.31 | 26 | 30.25 | 31 | −0.75 |
| 1983 | 30.25 | 31 | 30.40 | ? | ? |

(All calculations are rounded to two decimal places.)

In 1974 no forecasts or observations are available. In 1975 no old forecast is available and the new forecast is simply the latest observation (1974 sales).

In 1976, for example:

New forecast $= \alpha \times$ Latest information $+ (1-\alpha) \times$ Old forecast,
i.e., 1976 forecast $= 0.2 \times 1975$ sales $+ 0.8 \times 1975$ forecast,
i.e., 1976 forecast $= 0.2 \times 34 + 0.8 \times 35 = 34.8$.

The actual 1976 sales are given as 36 – an error of $-1.2$ in the prediction.

To predict this year's sales, only two numbers have to be available – last year's forecast of 30.40 and last year's actual sales, when known. In this method of forecasting, the original analysis does not have to be repeated every year (unlike the method of regression).

The choice of the value of the smoothing constant is the crucial part of the technique. When a number of observations are already available, it is possible to select the value of $\alpha$ which reduces the errors to a minimum. It is usual to find the sum of the squares of the errors and minimize this. The best value of $\alpha$ would be very difficult to evaluate by hand but could easily be found on a computer.

Very sophisticated versions of exponential smoothing have been developed. They use the above technique many times over to improve the accuracy of the predictions.

# Chapter 7

# Further Tests of Significance

In this chapter the $\chi^2$ test, the $F$-test and the analysis of variance will be considered.

## $\chi^2$ DISTRIBUTION

This distribution is used when a comparison of *frequencies* is appropriate.

A market research agency asked a sample of 500 people to classify one of three brands of a food product. The results are given below.

|  | Brand $A$ | Brand $B$ | Brand $C$ | Total |
|---|---|---|---|---|
| Dislike | 62 | 32 | 76 | 170 |
| Indifferent | 64 | 47 | 99 | 210 |
| Like | 24 | 21 | 75 | 120 |
| Total | 150 | 100 | 250 | 500 |

For example, of the 250 people who were asked to classify Brand $C$, 99 people were indifferent to it.

The table above is called a $3 \times 3$ **contingency table**. The entries under the brand types are called the **observed frequencies**.

The $\chi^2$ (chi-square) test is used to test the independence of the two factors – brand and personal taste. The apparent differences between the brands may be due to the fluctuations of random sampling, or there may well be a real difference between them.

*Null* hypothesis: The two factors are independent.

*Alternative* hypothesis: The two factors are dependent, i.e., a degree of association exists.

Under the assumption of independence, the **expected frequencies** have to be calculated and compared with the observed frequencies. The table of expected frequencies has the same row and column totals as the table above.

The following argument can be used to calculate the expected number of people disliking Brand $A$.

150 people were asked to classify Brand $A$.
170 people out of 500 indicated dislike.
Therefore, the expected number of people disliking Brand $A$ is:

$$\frac{170}{500} \times 150 = 51.$$

Alternatively, probabilities can be used.

$$P(\text{classified Brand } A) = \frac{150}{500}.$$

$$P(\text{indicated dislike}) = \frac{170}{500}.$$

$$P(\text{disliked Brand } A) = \frac{150}{500} \times \frac{170}{500} = 0.102.$$

By independence and the multiplication law, the expected number of people (out of 500) disliking Brand $A$ is:

$$500 \times 0.102 = 51.$$

In practice, the quickest method of finding the expected frequencies is to use the formula:

$$\text{Expected frequency} = \frac{\text{Row total} \times \text{Column total}}{\text{Grand total}}$$

A table of expected frequencies under independence is given below.

|  | A | B | C |  |
|---|---|---|---|---|
| Dislike | $\dfrac{170 \times 150}{500}$ $= 51*$ | $\dfrac{170 \times 100}{500}$ $= 34*$ | $\dfrac{170 \times 250}{500}$ $= 85$ | 170 |
| Indifferent | $\dfrac{210 \times 150}{500}$ $= 63*$ | $\dfrac{210 \times 100}{500}$ $= 42*$ | $\dfrac{210 \times 250}{500}$ $= 105$ | 210 |
| Like | $\dfrac{120 \times 150}{500}$ $= 36$ | $\dfrac{120 \times 100}{500}$ $= 24$ | $\dfrac{120 \times 250}{500}$ $= 60$ | 120 |
|  | 150 | 100 | 250 | 500 |

If the four asterisked frequencies in the table are calculated first, the remaining five values can be deduced from the row and column totals by subtraction. The number of asterisked frequencies, in this case four, is called the number of **degrees of freedom** and is required later for the $\chi^2$ test.

A measure of the difference between the observed and expected frequencies is given by:

$$\chi^2 = \Sigma \frac{(o-e)^2}{e}$$

where $o$ represents the observed frequencies,
         $e$ represents the corresponding expected frequencies.

The summation is made over all entries in the tables.

Thus $\chi^2 = \dfrac{(62-51)^2}{51} + \dfrac{(32-34)^2}{34} + \dfrac{(76-85)^2}{85} +$

$$\dfrac{(64-63)^2}{63} + \dfrac{(47-42)^2}{42} + \dfrac{(99-105)^2}{105} +$$

$$\dfrac{(24-36)^2}{36} + \dfrac{(21-24)^2}{24} + \dfrac{(75-60)^2}{60}$$

$$= 12.52$$

This measure of the difference is known to have a distribution which corresponds very closely to the $\chi^2$ distribution, when the grand total is greater than 50 and most expected frequencies are greater than ten (one or two may be allowed to fall a little below ten). The $\chi^2$ distribution has been tabulated on page 119 and is illustrated in Figure 31.

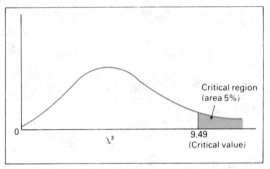

Figure 31. $\chi^2$ distribution with four degrees of freedom

The curve is skewed and only appears on the right-hand side of the vertical axis.

For a contingency table with $m$ rows and $n$ columns, the relevant degrees of freedom $v$ is given by:

$$v = (m-1)(n-1)$$

In this example, $v = (3-1)(3-1) = 2 \times 2 = 4$, as noted before.

Only large values of $\chi^2$ can upset the null hypothesis – this is always a one-tail test. From tables, the 5% point at four degrees of freedom is 9.49. Since the observed value of $\chi^2$ (12.52) lies in the critical region, the result is significant at the 5% level. In other words, the evidence suggests that there is a real difference between the three brands of the product.

### Example

The incidence of a particular industrial disease during a certain year is shown in the table below, both for people with protection against the disease and for people without any protection.

|              | No. without the disease | No. with the disease | Total |
|--------------|:-----------------------:|:--------------------:|:-----:|
| Protected    | 85                      | 11                   | 96    |
| Unprotected  | 228                     | 41                   | 269   |
| Total        | 313                     | 52                   | 365   |

Does this evidence support the view that the form of protection used reduces the incidence of the disease?

The expected frequency for the number of protected people not contracting the disease is:

$$\frac{96 \times 313}{365} = 82.32 \text{ to two decimal places.}$$

The remaining expected frequencies are then calculated by subtraction.

|              | No. without the disease | No. with the disease | Total |
|--------------|:-----------------------:|:--------------------:|:-----:|
| Protected    | 82.32                   | $96 - 82.32 = 13.68$ | 96    |
| Unprotected  | $313 - 82.32 = 230.68$  | $52 - 13.68 = 38.32$ | 269   |
| Total        | 313                     | 52                   | 365   |

$$\chi^2 = \frac{(85 - 82.32)^2}{82.32} + \frac{(11 - 13.68)^2}{13.68} + \frac{(228 - 230.68)^2}{230.68} +$$

$$\frac{(41 - 38.32)^2}{38.32}$$

$$= 0.0872 + 0.5250 + 0.0311 + 0.1874$$

$$= 0.83 \text{ to two decimal places.}$$

The number of degrees of freedom $v = (2-1)(2-1) = 1$. The critical value at the 5 % level is 3.84.

The result is not significant at the 5 % level. There is no clear evidence that the protection reduces the incidence of the disease. The conclusion does not imply that this form of protection should be abandoned. The statistical test indicates only that the observed frequencies could have reasonably arisen by chance under the hypothesis of independence, i.e., the incidence of the disease is the same for both protected and unprotected people. Other considerations, such as medical evidence, might well be much more important than statistical evidence.

## GOODNESS OF FIT

The $\chi^2$ distribution may also be used to test whether or not a set of observed frequencies is consistent with a given probability distribution. For example, it was claimed that the arrival of calls at a switchboard followed a Poisson distribution (see page 61). The following data are given from observations of 100 minutes at a switchboard.

| Number of calls per minute | Observed frequency ($f$) | $fx$ |
|---|---|---|
| 0 | 14 | 0 |
| 1 | 30 | 30 |
| 2 | 27 | 54 |
| 3 | 12 | 36 |
| 4 | 10 | 40 |
| 5 | 6 | 30 |
| 6 | 1 | 6 |
| | 100 | 196 |

To fit a Poisson distribution to this data, the value of the parameter $\mu$ (see page 61) has to be determined. Since $\mu$ is the mean, the best estimate of it is the sample mean $\bar{x}$.

$$\bar{x} = \frac{\Sigma fx}{\Sigma f} = \frac{196}{100} = 1.96.$$

The probabilities are now evaluated using the Poisson formula with $\mu = 1.96$:

| | | |
|---|---|---|
| $P(0) = 0.141$ | $P(3) = 0.177$ | $P(5) = 0.034$ |
| $P(1) = 0.276$ | $P(4) = 0.087$ | $P(6) = 0.011$ |
| $P(2) = 0.271$ | | |

Therefore, $P(7 \text{ or more}) = 0.003$, by using the fact that all the probabilities add up to one.

The expected frequencies are obtained by multiplying these probabilities by the total frequency of 100.

| Number of calls per minute | Observed frequency ($o$) | Expected frequency ($e$) | $\dfrac{(o-e)^2}{e}$ |
|---|---|---|---|
| 0 | 14 | 14.1 | 0.0007 |
| 1 | 30 | 27.6 | 0.2087 |
| 2 | 27 | 27.1 | 0.0004 |
| 3 | 12 | 17.7 | 1.8356 |
| 4 | 10 ⎫ | 8.7 ⎫ | |
| 5 | 6 ⎪ 4 or | 3.4 ⎪ | |
| 6 | 1 ⎬ more  17 | 1.1 ⎬ 13.5 | 0.9074 |
| 7 | 0 ⎭ | 0.3 ⎭ | |
| | 100 | 100.0 | 2.9528 |

The agreement is fairly close but, to decide how close, the $\chi^2$ value must be evaluated.

Since some of the expected frequencies are less than ten, the last four entries in each column have been added together to form the group, 4 or more (see the proviso on page 97). Note that $\chi^2 = 2.9528$, from the final column.

The calculation of the number of degrees of freedom proceeds as follows. (Note that the above table is *not* a contingency table.)

**1.** Find the number of expected frequencies used in the calculation of $\chi^2$.

This is five, from the last column of the table.

**2.** For every **constraint** satisfied by the observed and expected frequencies, reduce this number by one.

Since both sets of frequencies add up to the same total, this reduces the number to $5 - 1 = 4$.

Since both sets of frequencies have the same mean, because $\mu = 1.96$ and $\bar{x} = 1.96$, this reduces the number to $4 - 1 = 3$.

**3.** The degrees of freedom $v = 3$, i.e.,

$v$ = number of expected frequencies − number of constraints.

At three degrees of freedom, the critical value (at the 5% level) is 7.81. This is not significant so the observed data is consistent with that expected from a Poisson distribution of mean 1.96. Predictions based on this theoretical model of a switchboard can be made with some confidence.

*Note* Fitting a normal distribution to a set of grouped data would increase the number of constraints to three, because the sample standard deviation would also be needed to calculate the normal probabilities.

### Example
Fit a normal distribution to the following data and test for goodness of fit.

| Weight of product | Frequency | Weight of product | Frequency |
|---|---|---|---|
| 45–47 | 9 | 55–57 | 77 |
| 47–49 | 20 | 57–59 | 40 |
| 49–51 | 51 | 59–61 | 19 |
| 51–53 | 83 | 61–63 | 4 |
| 53–55 | 97 | | |

Total frequency $\quad n = 400$.

Arithmetic mean $\quad \bar{x} = \dfrac{9 \times 46 + 20 \times 48 + \ldots}{400} = 53.745$.

Variance $\quad s^2 = \dfrac{9 \times (46 - 53.745)^2 + \ldots}{400} = 10.765$.

Standard deviation $\quad s = \sqrt{10.765} = 3.281$.

(Full calculations have been omitted for the sake of brevity.)

A normal distribution, with a mean of 53.745 and an S.D. of 3.281, has now to be fitted. To find the expected frequency for the range 53 to 55, for example, the following procedure is used.

$$z_1 = \frac{53 - 53.745}{3.281} = -0.23 \text{ (number of S.D.s from the mean)}.$$

$A_1$ = area up to 53 = $1 - 0.5910 = 0.4090$ (from page 118).

$$z_2 = \frac{55 - 53.745}{3.281} = 0.38 \text{ (number of S.D.s from the mean)}.$$

$A_2$ = area up to 55 = 0.6480.
Area between 53 and 55 = $0.6480 - 0.4090 = 0.2390$.
Expected frequency = $400 \times 0.2390 = 95.6$.

The remaining frequencies are given below.

| | Area | e | o | $\chi^2$ |
|---|---|---|---|---|
| | | | 0 | 0.153 |
| 45–47 | 0.0159 | 6.4 | 9 | |
| 47–49 | 0.0538 | 21.5 | 20 | 0.105 |
| 49–51 | 0.1270 | 50.8 | 51 | 0.001 |
| 51–53 | 0.2085 | 83.4 | 83 | 0.002 |
| 53–55 | 0.2390 | 95.6 | 97 | 0.021 |
| 55–57 | 0.1909 | 76.4 | 77 | 0.005 |
| 57–59 | 0.1063 | 42.5 | 40 | 0.147 |
| 59–61 | 0.0412 | 16.5 | 19 | 0.379 |
| 61–63 | 0.0112 | 4.5 | 4 | 0.409 |
| >63 | 0.0024 | 1.0 | 0 | |
| | | | | 1.222 |

The first two groups and the last two groups have been combined – only two expected frequencies are now below ten.

Degrees of freedom $v$ = no. of frequencies − no. of constraints
$$= 9 - 3 = 6.$$

The critical value (5 % level) is 12.59.

The result is not significant. The data are consistent with those expected from a normal distribution. In fact, it would not be unreasonable to suspect the observations because the two sets of frequencies are so close together.

## F-DISTRIBUTION

This distribution is used to test whether two sample variances differ significantly. In the example on page 78, the following sample values are given.

Sample 1   Size 14   S.D.   10.61   Variance   112.57
Sample 2   Size 16   S.D.   12.42   Variance   154.26
(The variance is the square of the standard deviation.)

*Null* hypothesis: the two samples are drawn from normal distributions with the same population variance.
*Alternative* hypothesis: the two samples are drawn from normal distributions with differing population variances.

The critical ratio $F$ in this test is the ratio of the two sample variances, with the *larger variance in the numerator*.

$$F = \frac{154.26}{112.57} = 1.37.$$

The $F$-distribution has the following two **parameters**:

**1.** $v_1$ is the number of degrees of freedom of the *larger* variance, i.e., $v_1 = 16 - 1 = 15$ (one less than the size of the sample with the larger variance).

**2.** $v_2$ is the number of degrees of freedom of the *smaller* variance, i.e., $v_2 = 14 - 1 = 13$.

The function is tabulated on page 120 and illustrated in Figure 32.

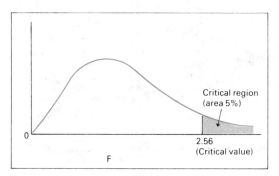

*Figure 32. F-distribution with parameters 15, 13*

$F$ is always positive and the test is always a one-tail test – larger values of $F$ discredit the null hypothesis.

The critical value (5% level) = 2.56, approximately, using the row with $v_2 = 13$ and estimating the value for $v_1 = 15$ from the columns headed $v_1 = 12$ and $v_1 = 24$.

The observed $F$ value of 1.37 is therefore not significant at the 5% level. The null hypothesis is accepted; the difference in sample variances is consistent with that obtained using random samples from normal distributions with the same variance.

## SIMPLE ANALYSIS OF VARIANCE

Three different fertilizers were tested on a particular crop to compare their performances. Each fertilizer was spread on four plots and the following yields obtained.

| Fertilizer | $A$ | $B$ | $C$ | |
|---|---|---|---|---|
| Yields | 7<br>4<br>5<br>4 | 1<br>5<br>4<br>6 | 6<br>6<br>5<br>7 | |
| Mean yield | 5 | 4 | 6 | 5 (grand mean) |

**Analysis of variance** (ANOVA) will test whether the difference between the mean yields is significant. It is also possible to apply three different $t$-tests for the difference between sample means (see page 77), but this can be tedious when there are a large number of means. Analysis of variance measures the types of variation that can arise in sampling experiments. In this example, there are two sources of variation.

**1.** Variation due to the differing properties of the fertilizers, i.e., variation *between* fertilizers.

**2.** Variation due to the difference in plots and the effects of sampling, i.e., variation *within* fertilizers – sometimes called the **residual variation**.

The table below shows these factors isolated.

| $A$ | $B$ | $C$ | | $A$ | $B$ | $C$ | | $A$ | $B$ | $C$ |
|---|---|---|---|---|---|---|---|---|---|---|
| 5 | 4 | 6 | | 2 | $-3$ | 0 | | 7 | 1 | 6 |
| 5 | 4 | 6 | | $-1$ | 1 | 0 | | 4 | 5 | 6 |
| 5 | 4 | 6 | | 0 | 0 | $-1$ | | 5 | 4 | 5 |
| 5 | 4 | 6 | | $-1$ | 2 | 1 | | 4 | 6 | 7 |
| Fertilizer yield (mean 5) | | | | Residual yield (mean 0) | | | | Total yield (mean 5) | | |

Each yield is split into two parts. The left-hand table shows the part that can be attributed to differences between fertilizers, i.e., the mean yields for each fertilizer. The middle table shows the *residual* yield, i.e., the actual yields in the right-hand table minus the mean yields in the left-hand table. A measure of the variations is now determined by finding the sum of the squared deviations from the mean, for each of the above tables.

Between variety **sum of squares**
$$= 4 \times (5-5)^2 + 4 \times (4-5)^2 + 4 \times (6-5)^2$$
$$= 8 \text{ (from the left-hand table with its grand mean of 5)}.$$

Residual sum of squares
$$= (2-0)^2 + (-3-0)^2 + (0-0)^2 + \ldots$$
$$= 4+9+0+1+1+0+0+0+1+1+4+1 = 22.$$
(from the middle table with its grand mean of 0).

Total sum of squares
$$= (7-5)^2 + (1-5)^2 + (6-5)^2 + \dots$$
$$= 4+16+1+1+0+1+0+1+0+1+1+4 = 30,$$
(from the right-hand table with its grand mean of 5).

As a check, the sum of the first two sums of squares should equal the total sum of squares $(8+22 = 30)$. The results are summarized below.

| Source of variation | Sum of squares (S.S.) | Degrees of freedom (D.F.) | Mean square (M.S.) | $F$ |
|---|---|---|---|---|
| Fertilizers | 8 | 2 | $8/2 = 4$ | 1.64 |
| Residual | 22 | 9 | $22/9 = 2.44$ | – |
| Total | 30 | 11 | $30/11 = 2.73$ | – |

The total degrees of freedom is one less than the number of observations, i.e., $12-1 = 11$ (see page 76).

The between variety degrees of freedom is one less than the number of fertilizers, i.e., $3-1 = 2$.

The residual degrees of freedom is therefore $11-2 = 9$, by subtraction.

The **mean square** in each row is evaluated by dividing the **sum of squares** by the degrees of freedom (these will not total properly).

The null hypothesis for this test is that the variation in yields can be accounted for by random sampling. Under this assumption, the three mean squares are all estimates of the population variance. The null hypothesis is rejected if the mean square between varieties is significantly *larger* than the residual mean square. For this purpose, the $F$-test of the last section may be used:

$$F = \frac{\text{Between variety M.S.}}{\text{Residual M.S.}} = \frac{4}{2.44} = 1.64,$$

at $v_1 = 2$, $v_2 = 9$ degrees of freedom.

The 5% point is 4.26, from page 119. This result is not significant – there is no evidence that the fertilizers produce different yields.

*Note:* If the observed $F$ value is *less* than one there is no need to exchange the mean squares to obtain a value larger than one. In such a case, the null hypothesis is accepted, since the variation between samples has to be significantly *larger* than that within samples to upset the null hypothesis.

### Notes on calculation of $F$ value
**1.** The final $F$ value is unaltered if the observations are coded initially.

**2.** The following method of calculation is often quicker.

| A | B | C |
|---|---|---|
| 7 | 1 | 6 |
| 4 | 5 | 6 |
| 5 | 4 | 5 |
| 4 | 6 | 7 |
| 20 | 16 | 24 |

Grand total $T = 20 + 16 + 24 = 60$.

**Correction factor** (C.F.) $= \dfrac{T^2}{12} = \dfrac{3600}{12} = 300$,

i.e., the grand total squared, divided by the number of observations.

**Crude sum of squares** $S = 7^2 + 1^2 + 6^2 + \ldots = 330$.
Total sum of squares $= S - C.F. = 330 - 300 = 30$, as before.

$$\text{Between sample sum of squares} = \frac{20^2 + 16^2 + 24^2}{4} - C.F.$$

$$= \frac{400 + 256 + 576}{4} - 300$$

$$= 8,$$

i.e., the sum of the squares of the sample totals, divided by the number in each sample, and minus the correction factor. The residual sum of squares $= 30 - 8 = 22$, by subtraction.

## TWO-WAY CLASSIFICATION

The analysis of variance is a very powerful technique. In an experiment with many factors, ANOVA isolates the variation that can be attributed to each factor, allowing an objective comparison of the differences within the factors. For example, if a tire company has to test different brands of tire, it must be ensured that all extraneous influences are isolated and discounted. The experiment might be designed to find the life of each kind of tire by driving them to destruction on a practice circuit. Factors that might affect the results are the type of car used, the driver's ability, the weather conditions and the speed of the car. In the next example, it is assumed that the same model of car is used, the speed is constant throughout the tests and the weather conditions are reasonably constant. This will, to a large extent, remove the effect of three factors, thus leaving two factors – type of tire and driver ability – to be allowed for.

Five different drivers test four types of tire, and the following table shows the life of the tires (data already coded).

| Driver | Tire | | | | Total |
| | A | B | C | D | |
|--------|-----|-----|-----|-----|-------|
| 1 | 0 | 53 | 3 | 72 | 128 |
| 2 | 2 | 75 | 20 | 89 | 186 |
| 3 | 26 | 92 | 42 | 70 | 230 |
| 4 | 27 | 57 | 54 | 91 | 229 |
| 5 | 28 | 78 | 78 | 94 | 278 |
| Total | 83 | 355 | 197 | 416 | 1051 (Grand total) |

The apparent difference between the four makes of tire, $A$, $B$, $C$ and $D$, might well be due to the difference between the five drivers, 1, 2, 3, 4 and 5, or it might be consistent with random sampling fluctuations. An exact analysis must be made to test this. Using the formulae expressed on page 105.

Grand total $T = 1051$.

Correction factor $= \dfrac{T^2}{20} = \dfrac{1051^2}{20} = 55\,230$.

Crude sum of squares
$S = 0^2 + 53^2 + 3^2 + 72^2 + \ldots = 74\,719$.
Total sum of squares
$S - \text{C.F.} = 74\,719 - 55\,230 = 19\,489$.

Degrees of freedom $= 20 - 1 = 19$ (one less than the number of observations).

Between tires S.S. $= \dfrac{83^2 + 355^2 + 197^2 + 416^2}{5} - 55\,230$
$$= 13\,726,$$

using the tire totals (five observations on each kind of tire).

Degrees of freedom $= 4 - 1 = 3$ (one less than the kinds of tire).

Between drivers S.S.

$$= \dfrac{128^2 + 186^2 + 230^2 + 229^2 + 278^2}{4} - 55\,230 = 3171,$$

using the driver totals (four observations for each driver).
Degrees of freedom $= 5 - 1 = 4$ (one less than the number of drivers).

The *analysis of variance table* is given below.

| Source | S.S. | D.F. | M.S. | F |
|--------|------|------|------|-----|
| Tires | 13 726 | 3 | 4575 | 21.2 |
| Drivers | 3 171 | 4 | 793 | 3.7 |
| Residual | 2 592 | 12 | 216 | — |
| Total | 19 489 | 19 | 1026 | — |

The residual S.S. and D.F. have been found by subtraction. The mean square (M.S.) is the sum of squares (S.S.) divided by the degrees of freedom (D.F.).

To test the significance of the variation between tires, the ratio below is found:

$$F = \frac{\text{Between tires M.S.}}{\text{Residual M.S.}} = \frac{4575}{216} = 21.2,$$

with $v_1 = 3$, $v_2 = 12$.

This is very significant at the 5 % level (critical value 3.49) and it may be concluded that there is a difference between the types of tire. Types $B$ and $D$ have a longer life than types $A$ and $C$, from the tire totals.

Similarly, for drivers:

$$F = \frac{\text{Between drivers M.S.}}{\text{Residual M.S.}} = \frac{793}{216} = 3.7,$$

with $v_1 = 4$, $v_2 = 12$.

This is significant at the 5 % level (critical value 3.26) and there is evidence of a difference between the performance of the drivers. From the driver totals, Driver number 5 appears to be less destructive on tires than Driver 1, for example. It is very unlikely that this difference has occurred by chance, e.g., Driver 1 receiving substandard tires.

*Note* The specimens of each type of tire must be allotted to the drivers at random. It has been assumed that there are no **interaction** effects between the factors. This interaction can be measured in some experiments but it is beyond the scope of this book.

## THREE-WAY CLASSIFICATION

When three factors have to be taken into account, the number of observations needed can be very large, especially if each factor has many levels. The next experiment uses a **Latin Square** design to reduce the number of data values required.

Four men are to weave four different kinds of yarn on four different machines. The breakage rates of the yarns and the design of the experiment are shown below.

|       | Machine 1 | Machine 2 | Machine 3 | Machine 4 |
|-------|-----------|-----------|-----------|-----------|
| Man $a$ | 5.4 ($A$) | 3.7 ($B$) | 9.3 ($C$) | 6.7 ($D$) |
| Man $b$ | 6.1 ($D$) | 6.2 ($A$) | 5.2 ($B$) | 9.2 ($C$) |
| Man $c$ | 8.7 ($C$) | 2.7 ($D$) | 5.5 ($A$) | 6.6 ($B$) |
| Man $d$ | 5.9 ($B$) | 5.1 ($C$) | 3.1 ($D$) | 8.3 ($A$) |

For example, yarn $A$ is woven on machine 1 by man $a$, on

machine 2 by man $b$ and so on. The Latin Square design (the letters in brackets) has been used to assign the kinds of yarn to men and machines. Note that every man and every machine works with each kind of yarn at some stage. The number of observations needed is 16, compared to the 64 which would be needed in a full experiment where every man weaves each yarn on each machine. This technique can only be applied when all of the factors have the same number of **levels**. The analysis of variance calculations proceed in a similar fashion to those of the last section in both a full experiment and a reduced experiment.

There are four sources of variation: between men; between machines; between yarns; and residual.

Totals for each machine    26.1, 17.7, 23.1, 30.8 $(1, 2, 3, 4)$.
Totals for each man        25.1, 26.7, 23.5, 22.4 $(a, b, c, d)$.
Totals for each yarn       25.4, 21.4, 32.3, 18.6 $(A, B, C, D)$.

Grand total $= 97.7$, from any one of the above totals.

Correction factor $= 97.7^2/16 = 596.58$.
Crude S.S. $= 5.4^2 + 3.7^2 + 9.3^2 + 6.7^2 + \ldots = 657.67$.
Total S.S. $= 657.67 - 596.58 = 61.09$ (D.F. 15).
Between machine S.S.
$= 0.25(26.1^2 + 17.7^2 + 23.1^2 + 30.8^2) - 596.58$
$= 22.61$ (D.F. 3).
Between men S.S.
$= 0.25(25.1^2 + 26.7^2 + 23.5^2 + 22.4^2) - 596.58$
$= 2.65$ (D.F. 3).
Between yarns S.S.
$= 0.25(25.4^2 + 21.4^2 + 32.3^2 + 18.6^2) - 596.58$
$= 26.51$ (D.F. 3).

The analysis of variances (ANOVA) table is shown below.

| Source | S.S. | D.F. | M.S. | $F$ |
|--------|------|------|------|-----|
| Machines | 22.61 | 3 | 7.54 | $7.54/1.55 = 4.86$ |
| Men | 2.65 | 3 | 0.88 | Not significant |
| Yarns | 26.51 | 3 | 8.84 | $8.84/1.55 = 5.70$ |
| Residual | 9.32 | 6 | 1.55 | — |
| Total | 61.09 | 15 | 4.07 | — |

The 5% point for $v_1 = 3, v_2 = 6$ is 4.76. There is a significant difference between machines (number 2 may be faulty) and between yarns ($D$ has a low breakage rate) but not between men (the M.S. is less than the residual M.S.).

# Chapter 8

# Further Topics

## QUALITY CONTROL

Statistical quality control is a technique used in mass production to ensure the uniformity of the product. Variation in the dimensions of manufactured articles is unavoidable and **tolerance limits** may have to be adhered to. A full inspection of all articles, rejecting those outside tolerance limits, can be very costly, but it is possible to sample only 5 %, say, of the articles and be confident of detecting faults in the process. Suppose that the quantity to be controlled is the diameter of a certain component. The nominal diameter is 3 mm and the tolerance factor is ±0.5 mm. Sample sizes of five are to be inspected at regular intervals (sample sizes can be anywhere between two and ten in practice). The results of the first ten samples are given below.

| Number of sample | (1) | (2) | (3) | (4) | (5) |
|---|---|---|---|---|---|
| | 2.9 | 2.8 | 3.0 | 2.8 | 3.2 |
| | 3.0 | 2.7 | 3.0 | 3.1 | 3.1 |
| | 2.8 | 3.0 | 3.1 | 3.0 | 2.9 |
| | 2.9 | 3.2 | 2.8 | 3.1 | 3.0 |
| | 2.8 | 3.4 | 3.0 | 2.8 | 3.3 |
| Sample mean | 2.88 | 3.02 | 2.98 | 2.96 | 3.10 |
| Sample range | 0.2 | 0.7 | 0.3 | 0.3 | 0.4 |

| Number of sample | (6) | (7) | (8) | (9) | (10) |
|---|---|---|---|---|---|
| | 3.0 | 2.9 | 3.1 | 2.9 | 2.8 |
| | 3.1 | 3.0 | 3.2 | 2.7 | 2.9 |
| | 3.2 | 3.1 | 3.0 | 3.0 | 2.7 |
| | 2.9 | 3.3 | 2.8 | 3.2 | 2.9 |
| | 3.1 | 2.9 | 3.0 | 3.0 | 2.9 |
| Sample mean | 3.06 | 3.04 | 3.02 | 2.96 | 2.84 |
| Sample range | 0.3 | 0.4 | 0.4 | 0.5 | 0.2 |

The sample range is the largest diameter minus the smallest diameter in each sample. It is used to estimate the standard deviation of the population (assumed normal). A little accuracy is lost by not calculating the S.D. by the usual formula, but the range is adequate for quality control purposes and is much simpler to calculate.

Grand average of all ten samples, $X = \dfrac{2.88 + 3.02 + \ldots +}{10}$

$$= 2.986.$$

Mean range of all ten samples, $R = \dfrac{0.2 + 0.7 + \ldots +}{10}$

$$= 0.37.$$

The estimate of the population S.D.,
$\sigma = aR = 0.43 \times 0.37 = 0.159$, where $a$ is the statistical quality control constant tabulated below.

| $n$ | 2 | 3 | 4 | 5 | 6 | 7 | 8 | 9 | 10 |
|---|---|---|---|---|---|---|---|---|---|
| $a$ | 0.89 | 0.59 | 0.49 | 0.43 | 0.39 | 0.37 | 0.35 | 0.34 | 0.32 |

($n$ is the sample size.)

From page 71, the standard error of the mean of a sample

$$(\text{Size } 5) = \frac{\sigma}{\sqrt{n}} = \frac{0.159}{\sqrt{5}} = 0.071.$$

From normal tables, 95% of the population lies within 1.96 S.E. of the mean and 99.8% of the population lies within 3.09 S.E. of the mean, i.e., in this example:
95% of the sample means should lie within the range:
$2.986 \pm 1.96 \times 0.071 = 2.847$ to $3.125$, using $\bar{X}$ and the S.E. of the mean.
99.8% of the sample means should lie within the range:
$2.986 \pm 3.09 \times 0.071 = 2.767$ to $3.205$.

These limits are now plotted on a **control chart** as shown in Figure 33.

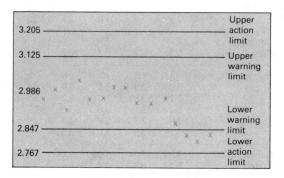

*Figure 33. Control chart for the mean of a sample*

Once the control chart is set up, the means of future samples of Size 5 are plotted on the diagram. If any point lies outside the **outer control lines**, action is taken. This will happen by chance 0.2% of the time (1 in 500 samples) so it is usual to take a few more samples. If any of these sample means lie outside the outer control lines, then the production manager can be almost certain that the machine is not functioning properly. The **inner control lines** are used as a warning of a possible fault that might be developing in the system. This is illustrated in the diagram where evidence of a fault is strong.

If the tolerance limits are of prime importance, it must be ensured that articles outside these limits are rejected. It is possible that the mean of a sample is within the outer control lines, yet one of its members is out of tolerance. For a single observation in the above example, 99.8 % of the diameters lie within the range $2.986 \pm 3.09 \times 0.159 = 2.495$ to $3.477$, using the population S.D., i.e., practically all the diameters lie in this range. If the tolerance range lies inside this range, the process will produce a high proportion of defectives which will not be detected by the control chart. This can be remedied in two ways – either by inspecting every component or by adjusting the machine in an attempt to reduce the standard deviation. In the present example, the tolerance range is 2.5 to 3.5 which can be maintained by the control chart.

By similar methods, it is possible to construct control charts for the range, the standard deviation and the proportion of defectives in a sample.

## SAMPLING INSPECTION

The technique of quality control helps the manufacturer to maintain standards. On the other hand, sampling inspection helps the buyer to estimate the quality of a batch of goods. The articles from production are assembled in **lots**, **batches** or **production runs**. A sample is then taken and the lot is either accepted or rejected on the basis of the sample. Total sampling (**screening**) can be too expensive or impractical if the testing is destructive. Some possible sampling schemes are shown below for articles which can be classified as good or defective.

**Single sample plan** Take a sample of $n$ articles. Count the number of defectives $x$.

**1.** Accept the lot if $x \leqslant c$.
**2.** Inspect the whole lot if $x > c$.
**3.** Replace all defectives found by good articles (usually at the producer's expense).

Here, $n$ and $c$ are numbers to be chosen from certain criteria.

**Double sample plan** Take a sample of $n$ articles ($x$ defective).

**1.** Accept the lot if $x \leqslant d$.
**2.** Take a second sample if $d < x \leqslant e$.
**3.** Reject the lot if $x > e$.

In the second case, another sample of size $m$ is taken ($y$ defective) and the following decisions are made.

**1.** Accept the lot if $x + y \leqslant e$.
**2.** Reject the lot if $x + y > e$.

($n$, $m$, $d$, $e$ have to be chosen.)

The double sample plan can be generalized to multiple samples and results in less sampling on average.

**Sequential analysis** In this plan, articles are selected at random one at a time. As soon as the number of defectives reaches a certain upper limit (in relation to the number sampled so far), the whole lot is rejected. If the number of defectives reaches a certain lower limit (in relation to the number sampled so far), the whole lot is accepted. Otherwise, the decision is to carry on sampling until one of the two limits is reached. The final sample size is thus determined by the results of earlier samples and is not initially specified.

The determination of the parameters of sampling plans is very much of a trial and error method. Extensive tables are available giving these parameters under specified conditions. The ideas behind the plans will be illustrated only in the single sample example.

**Single sample plan** Suppose that the size of the sample is 100, and the size of the lot is much greater than this number, so that the binomial distribution (see page 57) may be applied to the problem.

The **process average per cent defective** (PAPD) is the percentage (or proportion) of defective articles produced by the manufacturer. In practice, the producer will know this proportion from samples taken from the production line. On the other hand, the consumer does not want to base his sample plan on this figure, even if told it, because he may suspect that the producer is underestimating the proportion. The tables below give the probability of accepting the lot (**the operating characteristic**) for values of $c$ and $p$ (the PAPD).

| $p$ | 0.01 | 0.02 | 0.03 | 0.04 | 0.05 |
|---|---|---|---|---|---|
| $c$ | | | | | |
| 0 | 0.366 | 0.133 | 0.048 | 0.017 | 0.006 |
| 1 | 0.736 | 0.404 | 0.195 | 0.087 | 0.037 |
| 2 | 0.921 | 0.677 | 0.420 | 0.232 | 0.118 |
| 3 | 0.982 | 0.859 | 0.647 | 0.429 | 0.258 |

| $p$ | 0.06 | 0.07 | 0.08 | 0.09 | 0.10 |
|---|---|---|---|---|---|
| $c$ | | | | | |
| 0 | 0.002 | 0.001 | 0.000 | 0.000 | 0.000 |
| 1 | 0.015 | 0.006 | 0.002 | 0.001 | 0.000 |
| 2 | 0.056 | 0.026 | 0.011 | 0.005 | 0.002 |
| 3 | 0.142 | 0.075 | 0.036 | 0.018 | 0.008 |

For example, when $p = 0.01$, $c = 2$.

$P$(accepting the lot) $= P$(2 or less defectives in 100)
$= P(0) + P(1) + P(2)$
$= C_{100}^{0}(0.01)^{0}(0.99)^{100} + C_{100}^{1}(0.01)^{1}(0.99)^{99}$
$$+ C_{100}^{2}(0.01)^{2}(0.99)^{98}$$

$= 1 \times 1 \times 0.366 + 100 \times 0.01 \times 0.370 + 4950 \times 0.0001 \times 0.373$
$= 0.366 + 0.370 + 0.185$
$= 0.921$, using binomial probabilities.

The consumer has to choose the value of $c$ without knowing the value of $p$. His assessment of a good lot depends upon his **lot tolerance per cent defective** (LTPD). This figure is the maximum proportion of defectives that the consumer will tolerate. He can never guarantee that any lot he accepts will have a proportion of defectives less than his LTPD because it is possible that a sample might give an over-optimistic impression. The best that can be achieved (without 100% sampling) is to minimize the risk of accepting a bad lot (**the consumer's risk**).

Suppose that the consumer selects an LTPD of 0.05, i.e., the consumer would accept a lot with a proportion of defectives less than this figure. From the table headed $p = 0.05$:

When $c = 0$, $P$(accepting a bad lot) $= 0.006$.
When $c = 1$, $P$(accepting a bad lot) $= 0.037$.
When $c = 2$, $P$(accepting a bad lot) $= 0.118$.
When $c = 3$, $P$(accepting a bad lot) $= 0.258$.

If $c = 0$ is chosen, the consumer would only accept lots 36.6% of the time when $p$ is as low as 0.01. Similarly, a value of $c = 1$ would lead to a high rejection rate for good lots. In practice, a consumer's risk of around 10% is usual. The value to use is $c = 2$ for a sample size of 100 and the consumer's risk is 0.118. For values of $p$ larger than 0.05, the probabilities of accepting a bad lot in fact decrease (see table above). The consumer's risk is therefore a *conservative* estimate of the probability of accepting a bad lot without a full inspection. The sample plan is as follows.

**1.** Inspect a sample of 100 items.
**2.** If the number of defectives is less than or equal to 2, accept the lot.
**3.** Otherwise, inspect the whole lot.

Consumer's risk $= 0.118$, i.e., 11.8%.

The **producer's risk** under this scheme is the probability of the consumer rejecting a good lot and asking for a full screening. If the PAPD is 0.01 (known to the producer), from the tables the producer's risk is given as $1 - 0.921 = 0.079$, i.e., 7.9%.

The mean number of articles inspected (assuming a lot size of 1000) is $100 + 0.079 \times 900 = 171$, i.e., the initial sample of 100 plus the possibility of a full screening (probability 0.079) of the remaining 900 articles.

One method of deciding both the sample size and the value of $c$ proceeds as follows.

**1.** The consumer specifies his LTPD and the consumer's risk he is willing to accept. The producer specifies the lot size.

**2.** A series of values of $n$ and $c$ with the specified consumer's risk can then be determined from published tables.

**3.** The pair of values, $n$ and $c$, that minimize the average number of articles inspected is then selected from the list. This ensures that the cost of inspection is made as small as possible.

The **average outgoing quality** (AOQ) is the expected proportion of defectives in the lot after all the defectives found have been replaced by good articles. These values are tabulated below for various values of the PAPD.

| PAPD ($p$) | No. defectives (lot accepted) | Probability lot accepted | Expected no. defectives | AOQ(%) |
|------|------|------|------|------|
| 0.01 | 9  | 0.921 | 8.289  | 0.8289 |
| 0.02 | 18 | 0.677 | 12.186 | 1.2186 |
| 0.03 | 27 | 0.420 | 11.340 | 1.1340 |
| 0.04 | 36 | 0.232 | 8.352  | 0.8352 |
| 0.05 | 45 | 0.118 | 5.310  | 0.5310 |
| 0.06 | 54 | 0.056 | 3.024  | 0.3024 |
| 0.07 | 63 | 0.026 | 1.638  | 0.1638 |
| 0.08 | 72 | 0.011 | 0.792  | 0.0792 |
| 0.09 | 81 | 0.005 | 0.405  | 0.0405 |
| 0.10 | 90 | 0.002 | 0.180  | 0.0180 |

The second column gives the mean number of defectives when the lot is accepted – all defectives found in the initial sample of 100 are replaced by good articles but, on average, a proportion $p$ of the remaining 900 will be defective.

The third column values are found from the table on page 112 for $c = 2$.

The expected number of defectives in the lot when $p = 0.01$ is $9 \times 0.921 + 0 \times 0.079 = 8.289$, where 0.079 is the probability of the lot being rejected, resulting in a full screening which leaves zero defectives in the lot after replacement. The fourth column values are thus the product of the second and third column values.

The AOQ can then be calculated by dividing this latter column by 1000 to give a proportion, and then multiplying by 100 to give a percentage.

As far as the consumer is concerned, the PAPD is not known, but an inspection of the last column reveals that the worst AOQ under this sampling plan is 1.2186%. This is the **average outgoing quality limit** and occurs when $p = 0.02$. The consumer is therefore guaranteed a percentage of defectives no worse than about 1.2%. (This is a slight approximation because the highest AOQ might occur at a value of $p$, such as 0.018, which is not included in the table.) Paradoxically, if the producer begins to send in bad lots with a PAPD near to the LTPD (0.05), the consumer receives a better AOQ. This is due to the fact that full screening becomes more common, i.e., more lots are rejected on the basis of the initial sample. Since the inspection costs are usually paid by the producer, it is not in his interests to try to sell bad lots. The consumer is thus protected to a large extent as long as he is willing to take a slight risk of accepting a bad lot without full screening (the consumer's risk).

## RISK ANALYSIS

Uncertainty exists in many business situations. Risk analysis attempts to predict the possible outcomes of a project using subjective estimates of the probabilities. For example, a firm is considering the introduction of a product and the following estimates have been made.

| | | | |
|---|---|---|---|
| Fixed costs | $80 000 | $100 000 | $120 000 |
| Probability | 0.2 | 0.4 | 0.4 |
| Variable cost (per unit) | $3 | $4 | $5 |
| Probability | 0.2 | 0.5 | 0.3 |
| Sales quantity (selling price $6) | | 50 000 | 60 000 |
| Probability | | 0.4 | 0.6 |
| Sales quantity (selling price $5.50) | | 70 000 | 90 000 |
| Probability | | 0.5 | 0.5 |

The use of expected values (see page 50) can give the average profit for each of the two possible selling prices.

Expected fixed costs
    = 80 000 × 0.2 + 100 000 × 0.4 + 120 000 × 0.4
    = $104 000.
Expected variable cost = 3 × 0.2 + 4 × 0.5 + 5 × 0.3 = $4.1.

*Selling price $6*
Expected sales quantity
    = 50 000 × 0.4 + 60 000 × 0.6 = 56 000.
Expected profit = 56 000(6 − 4.1) − 104 000 = $2400.

*Selling price $5.50*
Expected sales quantity
    = 70 000 × 0.5 + 90 000 × 0.5 = 80 000.
Expected profit = 80 000(5.5 − 4.1) − 104 000 = $8000.

*Note* Strictly speaking, these expected profits are not exact, since the average value of the product of two quantities is not, in general, equal to the product of the averages of the two quantities.

This superficial analysis does not quantify the risk of the venture. Even though the expected profits are positive, it is possible to make a loss when the worst outcomes occur. A deeper analysis is needed to find the probability of this happening.

*For a selling price of $6*

| Fixed costs | Variable cost | Sales | Probability | Profit |
|---|---|---|---|---|
| 80 000 | 3 | 50 000 | 0.016 | 70 000 |
| 80 000 | 3 | 60 000 | 0.024 | 100 000 |
| 80 000 | 4 | 50 000 | 0.040 | 20 000 |
| 80 000 | 4 | 60 000 | 0.060 | 40 000 |
| 80 000 | 5 | 50 000 | 0.024 | −30 000 |
| 80 000 | 5 | 60 000 | 0.036 | −20 000 |
| 100 000 | 3 | 50 000 | 0.032 | 50 000 |
| 100 000 | 3 | 60 000 | 0.048 | 80 000 |
| 100 000 | 4 | 50 000 | 0.080 | 0 |
| 100 000 | 4 | 60 000 | 0.120 | 20 000 |
| 100 000 | 5 | 50 000 | 0.048 | −50 000 |
| 100 000 | 5 | 60 000 | 0.072 | −40 000 |
| 120 000 | 3 | 50 000 | 0.032 | 30 000 |
| 120 000 | 3 | 60 000 | 0.048 | 60 000 |
| 120 000 | 4 | 50 000 | 0.080 | −20 000 |
| 120 000 | 4 | 60 000 | 0.120 | 0 |
| 120 000 | 5 | 50 000 | 0.048 | −70 000 |
| 120 000 | 5 | 60 000 | 0.072 | −60 000 |

The table shows every possible combination of the variables. The probabilities have been calculated by multiplying the corresponding subjective probabilities.

For example, for the first row:
Probability $= 0.2 \times 0.2 \times 0.4 = 0.016$;
Profit $= 50\,000(6 - 3) - 80\,000 = \$70\,000$.

By adding together the relevant probabilities:
$P$(profit positive) $= 0.42$;
$P$(profit zero)      $= 0.20$;
$P$(profit negative) $= 0.38$;
i.e., there is a high risk of the venture losing money.

Similarly, for a selling price of $5.50:
$P$(profit zero)      $= 0.20$;
$P$(profit negative) $= 0.38$;
i.e., there is a high risk of the venture losing money.

Neither of the two options offers a good chance of a profit. The product is not worth introducing unless future developments reduce the costs, increase predicted sales or cause a reassessment of the probabilities.

## Example
A new project is to be launched and the following estimates of cash flows have been made.

|  | Year 1 | Year 2 | Year 3 | Probability |
|---|---|---|---|---|
| (a) | 70 000 | 100 000 | 150 000 | 0.1 |
| (b) | 65 000 | 90 000 | 120 000 | 0.5 |
| (c) | 65 000 | 80 000 | 100 000 | 0.4 |

| | Initial investment | Probability |
|---|---|---|
| (d) | 180 000 | 0.3 |
| (e) | 190 000 | 0.4 |
| (f) | 200 000 | 0.3 |

The cost of capital is 12%.

The net present value of the project for the most optimistic estimates is:

$$\text{NPV} = -180\,000 + \frac{70\,000}{1.12} + \frac{100\,000}{1.12^2} + \frac{150\,000}{1.12^3} = \$68\,986.$$

Probability $= 0.1 \times 0.3 = 0.03$.

The NPVs of the remaining outcomes can be calculated in a similar fashion.

| | | (d) 0.3 | (e) 0.4 | (f) 0.3 |
|---|---|---|---|---|
| (a) | 0.1 | 68 986 (0.03) | 58 986 (0.04) | 48 986 (0.03) |
| (b) | 0.5 | 35 197 (0.15) | 25 197 (0.20) | 15 197 (0.15) |
| (c) | 0.4 | 12 989 (0.12) | 2 989 (0.16) | −7 011 (0.12) |

From this table:
$P(\text{project losing money}) = 0.12$;
$P(\text{project gaining money}) = 0.88$.

The project is promising on the strength of this analysis. Unless the company is very **risk averse**, the venture is worth implementing (assuming that there are no other factors to be taken into consideration).

# Appendix

| | 0.00 | 0.01 | 0.02 | 0.03 | 0.04 | 0.05 | 0.06 | 0.07 | 0.08 | 0.09 |
|---|---|---|---|---|---|---|---|---|---|---|
| 0.0 | 5000 | 5040 | 5080 | 5120 | 5160 | 5199 | 5239 | 5279 | 5319 | 5359 |
| 0.1 | 5398 | 5438 | 5478 | 5517 | 5557 | 5596 | 5636 | 5675 | 5714 | 5753 |
| 0.2 | 5793 | 5832 | 5871 | 5910 | 5948 | 5987 | 6026 | 6064 | 6103 | 6141 |
| 0.3 | 6179 | 6217 | 6255 | 6293 | 6331 | 6368 | 6406 | 6443 | 6480 | 6517 |
| 0.4 | 6554 | 6591 | 6628 | 6664 | 6700 | 6736 | 6772 | 6808 | 6844 | 6879 |
| 0.5 | 6915 | 6950 | 6985 | 7019 | 7054 | 7088 | 7123 | 7157 | 7190 | 7224 |
| 0.6 | 7257 | 7291 | 7324 | 7357 | 7389 | 7422 | 7454 | 7486 | 7517 | 7549 |
| 0.7 | 7580 | 7612 | 7642 | 7673 | 7704 | 7734 | 7764 | 7794 | 7823 | 7852 |
| 0.8 | 7881 | 7910 | 7939 | 7967 | 7995 | 8023 | 8051 | 8078 | 8106 | 8133 |
| 0.9 | 8159 | 8186 | 8212 | 8238 | 8264 | 8289 | 8315 | 8340 | 8365 | 8389 |
| 1.0 | 8413 | 8438 | 8461 | 8485 | 8508 | 8531 | 8554 | 8577 | 8599 | 8621 |
| 1.1 | 8643 | 8665 | 8686 | 8708 | 8729 | 8749 | 8770 | 8790 | 8810 | 8830 |
| 1.2 | 8849 | 8869 | 8888 | 8907 | 8925 | 8944 | 8962 | 8980 | 8997 | 9015 |
| 1.3 | 9032 | 9049 | 9066 | 9082 | 9099 | 9115 | 9131 | 9147 | 9162 | 9177 |
| 1.4 | 9192 | 9207 | 9222 | 9236 | 9251 | 9265 | 9279 | 9292 | 9306 | 9319 |
| 1.5 | 9332 | 9345 | 9357 | 9370 | 9382 | 9394 | 9406 | 9418 | 9429 | 9441 |
| 1.6 | 9452 | 9463 | 9474 | 9484 | 9495 | 9505 | 9515 | 9525 | 9535 | 9545 |
| 1.7 | 9554 | 9564 | 9573 | 9582 | 9591 | 9599 | 9608 | 9616 | 9625 | 9633 |
| 1.8 | 9641 | 9649 | 9656 | 9664 | 9671 | 9678 | 9686 | 9693 | 9699 | 9706 |
| 1.9 | 9713 | 9719 | 9726 | 9732 | 9738 | 9744 | 9750 | 9756 | 9761 | 9767 |
| 2.0 | 9772 | 9778 | 9783 | 9788 | 9793 | 9798 | 9803 | 9808 | 9812 | 9817 |
| 2.1 | 9821 | 9826 | 9830 | 9834 | 9838 | 9842 | 9846 | 9850 | 9854 | 9857 |
| 2.2 | 9861 | 9864 | 9868 | 9871 | 9875 | 9878 | 9881 | 9884 | 9887 | 9890 |
| 2.3 | 9893 | 9896 | 9898 | 9901 | 9904 | 9906 | 9909 | 9911 | 9913 | 9916 |
| 2.4 | 9918 | 9920 | 9922 | 9925 | 9927 | 9929 | 9931 | 9932 | 9934 | 9936 |
| 2.5 | 9938 | 9940 | 9941 | 9943 | 9945 | 9946 | 9948 | 9949 | 9951 | 9952 |
| 2.6 | 9953 | 9955 | 9956 | 9957 | 9959 | 9960 | 9961 | 9962 | 9963 | 9964 |
| 2.7 | 9965 | 9966 | 9967 | 9968 | 9969 | 9970 | 9971 | 9972 | 9973 | 9974 |
| 2.8 | 9974 | 9975 | 9976 | 9977 | 9977 | 9978 | 9979 | 9979 | 9980 | 9981 |
| 2.9 | 9981 | 9982 | 9982 | 9983 | 9984 | 9984 | 9985 | 9985 | 9986 | 9986 |
| 3.0 | 9987 | 9987 | 9987 | 9988 | 9988 | 9989 | 9989 | 9989 | 9990 | 9990 |

*To find the area up to 2.63*
Find the row starting with 2.6 and the column headed 0.03. The corresponding entry is 9957, representing an area of 0.9957 or 99.57%.

*To find the area up to −1.93*
Find the entry for 1.93, i.e., 0.9732 and subtract from one, i.e., $1 - 0.9732 = 0.0268$.

*To find the 5% points for a two-tail test*
The area in each tail is 2.5%, i.e., 0.0250, so the area up to the positive critical value is $1 - 0.0250 = 0.9750$. Look up 9750 in the body of the table – this occurs under the entry 1.96. The 5% points are −1.96 and 1.96.

## 5% Points of the t-distribution (two-tail test)

v is the degrees of freedom

| v | 1 | 2 | 3 | 4 | 5 | 6 | 7 | 8 | 9 |
|---|---|---|---|---|---|---|---|---|---|
| | 12.71 | 4.30 | 3.18 | 2.78 | 2.57 | 2.45 | 2.37 | 2.31 | 2.26 |
| v | 10 | 11 | 12 | 13 | 14 | 15 | 16 | 17 | 18 |
| | 2.23 | 2.20 | 2.18 | 2.16 | 2.15 | 2.13 | 2.12 | 2.11 | 2.10 |
| v | 19 | 20 | 21 | 22 | 23 | 24 | 25 | 26 | 27 |
| | 2.09 | 2.09 | 2.08 | 2.07 | 2.07 | 2.06 | 2.06 | 2.06 | 2.05 |
| v | 28 | 29 | 30 | 40 | 60 | 120 | $\infty$ | | |
| | 2.05 | 2.05 | 2.04 | 2.02 | 2.00 | 1.98 | 1.96 | | |

The above table is taken from Table III of Fisher & Yates: *Statistical Tables for Biological, Agricultural and Medical Research* published by Longman Group Ltd., London (previously published by Oliver & Boyd Ltd., Edinburgh) and by permission of the authors and publishers.

## 5% points of the $\chi^2$ distribution (one-tail test)

v is the degrees of freedom

| v | 1 | 2 | 3 | 4 | 5 | 6 | 7 |
|---|---|---|---|---|---|---|---|
| | 3.84 | 5.99 | 7.81 | 9.49 | 11.07 | 12.59 | 14.07 |
| v | 8 | 9 | 10 | 11 | 12 | 13 | 14 |
| | 15.51 | 16.92 | 18.31 | 19.68 | 21.03 | 22.36 | 23.69 |
| v | 15 | 16 | 17 | 18 | 19 | 20 | 21 |
| | 25.00 | 26.30 | 27.59 | 28.87 | 30.14 | 31.41 | 32.67 |
| v | 22 | 23 | 24 | 25 | 26 | 27 | 28 |
| | 33.92 | 35.17 | 36.42 | 37.65 | 38.89 | 40.11 | 41.34 |
| v | 29 | 30 | | | | | |
| | 42.56 | 43.77 | | | | | |

The above table is taken from Table IV of Fisher & Yates: *Statistical Tables for Biological, Agricultural and Medical Research* published by Longman Group Ltd., London (previously published by Oliver & Boyd Ltd., Edinburgh) and by permission of the authors and publishers.

## 5% points of the F-distribution (one-tail test)

$v_1$ is the number of degrees of freedom of the larger variance.
$v_2$ is the number of degrees of freedom of the smaller variance.

| $v_2$ \ $v_1$ | 1 | 2 | 3 | 4 | 5 | 6 | 8 | 12 | 24 | $\infty$ |
|---|---|---|---|---|---|---|---|---|---|---|
| 1 | 161.4 | 199.5 | 215.7 | 224.6 | 230.2 | 234.0 | 238.9 | 243.9 | 249.0 | 254.3 |
| 2 | 18.51 | 19.00 | 19.16 | 19.25 | 19.30 | 19.33 | 19.37 | 19.41 | 19.45 | 19.50 |
| 3 | 10.13 | 9.55 | 9.28 | 9.12 | 9.01 | 8.94 | 8.84 | 8.74 | 8.64 | 8.53 |
| 4 | 7.71 | 6.94 | 6.59 | 6.39 | 6.26 | 6.16 | 6.04 | 5.91 | 5.77 | 5.63 |
| 5 | 6.61 | 5.79 | 5.41 | 5.19 | 5.05 | 4.95 | 4.82 | 4.68 | 4.53 | 4.36 |
| 6 | 5.99 | 5.14 | 4.76 | 4.53 | 4.39 | 4.28 | 4.15 | 4.00 | 3.84 | 3.67 |
| 7 | 5.59 | 4.74 | 4.35 | 4.12 | 3.97 | 3.87 | 3.73 | 3.57 | 3.41 | 3.23 |
| 8 | 5.32 | 4.46 | 4.07 | 3.84 | 3.69 | 3.58 | 3.44 | 3.28 | 3.12 | 2.93 |
| 9 | 5.12 | 4.26 | 3.86 | 3.63 | 3.48 | 3.37 | 3.23 | 3.07 | 2.90 | 2.71 |
| 10 | 4.96 | 4.10 | 3.71 | 3.48 | 3.33 | 3.22 | 3.07 | 2.91 | 2.74 | 2.54 |
| 11 | 4.84 | 3.98 | 3.59 | 3.36 | 3.20 | 3.09 | 2.95 | 2.79 | 2.61 | 2.40 |
| 12 | 4.75 | 3.88 | 3.49 | 3.26 | 3.11 | 3.00 | 2.85 | 2.69 | 2.50 | 2.30 |
| 13 | 4.67 | 3.80 | 3.41 | 3.18 | 3.02 | 2.92 | 2.77 | 2.60 | 2.42 | 2.21 |
| 14 | 4.60 | 3.74 | 3.34 | 3.11 | 2.96 | 2.85 | 2.70 | 2.53 | 2.35 | 2.13 |
| 15 | 4.54 | 3.68 | 3.29 | 3.06 | 2.90 | 2.79 | 2.64 | 2.48 | 2.29 | 2.07 |
| 16 | 4.49 | 3.63 | 3.24 | 3.01 | 2.85 | 2.74 | 2.59 | 2.42 | 2.24 | 2.01 |
| 17 | 4.45 | 3.59 | 3.20 | 2.96 | 2.81 | 2.70 | 2.55 | 2.38 | 2.19 | 1.96 |
| 18 | 4.41 | 3.55 | 3.16 | 2.93 | 2.77 | 2.66 | 2.51 | 2.34 | 2.15 | 1.92 |
| 19 | 4.38 | 3.52 | 3.13 | 2.90 | 2.74 | 2.63 | 2.48 | 2.31 | 2.11 | 1.88 |
| 20 | 4.35 | 3.49 | 3.10 | 2.87 | 2.71 | 2.60 | 2.45 | 2.28 | 2.08 | 1.84 |
| 21 | 4.32 | 3.47 | 3.07 | 2.84 | 2.68 | 2.57 | 2.42 | 2.25 | 2.05 | 1.81 |
| 22 | 4.30 | 3.44 | 3.05 | 2.82 | 2.66 | 2.55 | 2.40 | 2.23 | 2.03 | 1.78 |
| 23 | 4.28 | 3.42 | 3.03 | 2.80 | 2.64 | 2.53 | 2.38 | 2.20 | 2.00 | 1.76 |
| 24 | 4.26 | 3.40 | 3.01 | 2.78 | 2.62 | 2.51 | 2.36 | 2.18 | 1.98 | 1.73 |
| 25 | 4.24 | 3.38 | 2.99 | 2.76 | 2.60 | 2.49 | 2.34 | 2.16 | 1.96 | 1.71 |
| 26 | 4.22 | 3.37 | 2.98 | 2.74 | 2.59 | 2.47 | 2.32 | 2.15 | 1.95 | 1.69 |
| 27 | 4.21 | 3.35 | 2.96 | 2.73 | 2.57 | 2.46 | 2.30 | 2.13 | 1.93 | 1.67 |
| 28 | 4.20 | 3.34 | 2.95 | 2.71 | 2.56 | 2.44 | 2.29 | 2.12 | 1.91 | 1.65 |
| 29 | 4.18 | 3.33 | 2.93 | 2.70 | 2.54 | 2.43 | 2.28 | 2.10 | 1.90 | 1.64 |
| 30 | 4.17 | 3.32 | 2.92 | 2.69 | 2.53 | 2.42 | 2.27 | 2.09 | 1.89 | 1.62 |
| 40 | 4.08 | 3.23 | 2.84 | 2.61 | 2.45 | 2.34 | 2.18 | 2.00 | 1.79 | 1.51 |
| 60 | 4.00 | 3.15 | 2.76 | 2.52 | 2.37 | 2.25 | 2.10 | 1.92 | 1.70 | 1.39 |
| 120 | 3.92 | 3.07 | 3.68 | 2.45 | 2.29 | 2.17 | 2.02 | 1.83 | 1.61 | 1.25 |
| $\infty$ | 3.84 | 2.99 | 2.60 | 2.37 | 2.21 | 2.09 | 1.94 | 1.75 | 1.52 | 1.00 |

The above table is taken from Table V of Fisher & Yates: *Statistical Tables for Biological, Agricultural and Medical Research* published by Longman Group Ltd., London (previously published by Oliver & Boyd Ltd., Edinburgh) and by permission of the authors and publishers.

# Further Reading

De Groot, M., *Probability and Statistics* (Addison-Wesley, 1975)

Gregory, D. and Ward, H., *Statistics for Business Studies* (McGraw-Hill, 1978)

Hair, J., Anderson, R., Tatham, R., and Grablowsky, B., *Multivariate Data Analysis* (Petroleum Publishing Co., 1979)

Morrison, D., *Multivariate Statistical Methods* (McGraw-Hill, Second Edition, 1976)

Raiffa, H., and Schlaifer, R., *Applied Statistical Decision Theory* (Harvard, 1961)

Sudman, S., *Applied Sampling* (Academic Press, 1976)

Wheelwright, S., and Makridakis, S., *Forecasting Methods for Management* (Wiley, Second Edition, 1977)

# Glossary

**Acceptance region** The region of the sampling distribution in which the sample statistic value has to fall for the null hypothesis to be accepted (significance tests).

**Addition law** The law of probability relating to the disjunction of two or more events:

$$P(A \text{ or } B) = P(A) + P(B) - P(A \text{ and } B).$$

**Alternative hypothesis** The formulation of the population parameter(s) contradicting the null hypothesis. It is crucial to the determination of the critical region of a significance test.

**Analysis of variance** A statistical technique, developed by Fisher, to quantify and compare the sources of variation in an experiment.

**Arithmetic mean** The most commonly used measure of location. It is defined as the sum of a set of data values divided by the number of data values.

**Average** A general term for a measure of location such as the mean, median or mode although it tends to be loosely applied to the mean alone.

**Average outgoing quality** The expected proportion or percentage of defective articles in a lot after inspection.

**Bar chart** A frequency diagram used to represent grouped data. It consists of a number of rectangles, the heights of which correspond to the cell frequencies and the widths, all of which are equal, to the cell sizes (cf. histogram).

**Bayes' theorem** A probability law relating *a posteriori* probability to *a priori* probability.

**Bimodal** A frequency or probability distribution with two modes.

**Binomial distribution** The probability distribution relating to the number of 'successes' in any number of independent realizations of an event.

**Cartogram** A statistical map conveying information about geographical distributions such as population density, millimeters of rainfall, etc.

**Categorical data** Data sorted into groups according to some qualitative description, e.g., like, indifference, dislike.

**Chi-square distribution** A continuous probability distribution, formulated by Helmert and later discovered by Pearson, which approximates the sampling distribution of $\chi^2$ in the goodness of fit test and the contingency table test.

**Coding** A technique employed to simplify data values – the observations are reduced by some number and/or divided by some number.

**Coefficient of determination** The square of the correlation coefficient giving a measure of the amount of variation explained by the line of best fit.

**Coefficient of variation** A measure of the relative dispersion of a set of data values – the standard deviation divided by the arithmetic mean.

**Column chart** A frequency diagram used for the aggregates of observations (also known as a component bar chart).

**Combination** The number of selections of a given number of objects from a population where order is irrelevant and the choices are made without replacement.

**Complement** $(\bar{A})$ The outcome realized when the event $A$ does not happen.

**Conditional probability** The probability of an event given that some other event has occurred.

**Confidence interval** The range within which a population parameter is likely to lie as the result of a sampling experiment (usually a 95% confidence interval).

**Conjunction** The compound event, $A$ and $B$, where $A$, $B$ are two events.

**Consumer's risk** The probability of a bad lot being accepted by the consumer in a sample plan.

**Contingency table** A table representing the dichotomy of two factors by quoting the frequencies or probabilities.

**Continuous variable** A variable which may take any value in theory, such as the height of a person, the weight of an object, i.e., the values are not restricted to whole numbers.

**Control chart** A graph used to check and regulate the quantitative characteristics of articles from a production line.

**Correlation coefficient** A measure of the degree of linear association between two variables, first introduced by Galton.

**Covariance** A raw measure of linear association calculated by summing the product of the deviations from the mean of the two variables and dividing by the number of paired observations.

**Critical ratio** The observed standardized variate which is compared with the critical value to determine the significance or non-significance of a hypothesis test.

**Critical region** The area under the sampling distribution in which the sample statistic value has to fall for the null hypothesis to be rejected (significance tests).

**Critical value** The number on the border of the critical and acceptance regions.

**Cumulative frequency** The sum of all the frequencies to date. It is used in the construction of ogives.

**Curvilinear regression** A technique to fit curves to a set of observations.

**Decision node** A point on a decision tree leading to a set of possible decisions.

**Decision tree** A diagrammatic representation of the various decisions and outcomes of a project.

**Degrees of freedom** A general term used for the parameters of the $t$, $F$ and $\chi^2$ distributions.

**Dependent variable** The variable whose value is determined for given values of the independent variable. The regression line is used to predict values of this variable only.

**Direct correlation** The association between two variables when the correlation coefficient is positive, i.e., as one variable increases (decreases) the other tends to increase (decrease) as well.

**Discrete variable** A variable which can only take certain values, e.g., the size of a family must be a whole number.

**Disjunction** The compound event $A$ or $B$ representing the occurrence of either $A$ or $B$ or both.

**Dispersion** The general term for the "spread" of a distribution. It is commonly measured by the standard deviation, the range or the semi inter-quartile range.

**Euler number** The mathematical constant e (2.718 281 8) which appears in the equation of many probability distributions.

**Exhaustive** A set of events which contain every conceivable outcome.

**Expected value** The arithmetic mean of a variable, usually calculated from the frequency or probability distribution.

**Exponential function** The curve describing a variable which increases (decreases) by the same proportion during a constant time period.

**Exponential smoothing** A method used for short-term forecasting in which older observations are given less weight than more recent ones.

***F*-distribution** A continuous probability distribution used to test the equality of two population variances.

**Fiducial limit** Another term for a confidence limit.

**Frequency** The number of times that a value or range of values occurs in a set of observations.

**Frequency polygon** A graph constructed by joining the mid-points of each cell at the corresponding frequency.

**Gaussian curve** Another term for the normal curve.

**Geometric mean** A measure of location obtained by multiplying the data values together and taking the $n$th root where $n$ is the number of data values. It is rarely used although it does have applications in the construction of index numbers.

**Histogram** A frequency diagram used to represent grouped data. The area of the rectangles corresponds to the frequency and the cell widths need not be the same.

**Hypothesis test** *see* Significance test.

**Independent** Two events are said to be independent when the occurrence or non-occurrence of one of them does not affect the probability of the other occurring.

**Independent variable** The variable whose values are set before observations of the dependent variable are made. (Time is often the independent variable.)

**Indirect correlation** The association between two variables when the correlation coefficient is negative, i.e., as one variable increases (decreases) the other tends to decrease (increase).

**Inner control line** One of the two lines on a control chart which serves as a warning line. It is usually set at 1.96 standard errors from the mean.

**Kurtosis** A measure of the "flattening" of a distribution. A curve which is taller and thinner than the normal curve is called leptokurtic and one which is shorter and fatter than the normal curve is called platykurtic.

**Latin square** An experimental design used in analysis of variance tests to reduce the number of observations needed.

**Least squares method** The technique of fitting lines or curves to a set of paired observations, in which the sum of the squared deviations from the line (or curve) is made as small as possible.

**Level of significance** The probability which determines the critical region of a significance test. A result which is significant at the 5% level, for example, means that the probability of obtaining a sample statistic value as far from the mean as that observed is less than 5%. In this case the probability of a type I error is also 5%.

**Linear regression** The technique of fitting the line of best fit to a set of paired observations.

**Lot tolerance per cent defective** (LTPD) The maximum percentage of defectives in a lot that the consumer is willing to tolerate.

**Mean** A shorter (abbreviated) term for the arithmetic mean.

**Mean deviation** A measure of dispersion calculated by averaging the absolute deviations of the data values from the mean (or sometimes the median). It is easier to calculate than the standard deviation but leads to extremely complicated mathematical analysis.

**Mean square** The sum of squares of a factor divided by the number of degrees of freedom (ANOVA).

**Measure of central tendency** (also called measure of position). A general term for a statistic giving an indication of the "center" of a distribution, e.g., mean, median, mode.

**Median** The middle data value of a set of observations when written in increasing or decreasing order. The median bisects the area of the distribution.

**Minimax** A method of selecting one of several options in such a way that the minimum possible gain is made as large as possible.

**Mode** The value which occurs most frequently in a distribution. Sometimes called the norm.

**Monte Carlo method** A general term for techniques which use random numbers, e.g., simulation of a queuing system.

**Multilinear regression** A standard method of fitting lines in three or more dimensions to a set of multiple observations, e.g., finding the linear equation to predict sales from the two quantities, cost and advertising.

**Multiplication law** The law of probability relating to the conjunction of two or more events:

$$P(A \text{ and } B) = P(A) \times P(B/A) = P(B)p(A/B).$$

**Mutually exclusive** Two events are said to be mutually exclusive when the occurrence of one of them excludes the possibility of the other happening.

**Negative correlation** Another term for indirect correlation.

**Negative skew** The description of a distribution in which more than half of the area is to the left of the mode.

**Normal distribution** A continuous probability distribution of fundamental importance in statistical theory. Its curve is symmetrical and bell-shaped. Many variables such as length, weight and errors have a distribution which is normal or very nearly so.

**Null hypothesis** The statement of the value(s) of the population parameter(s) which is tested in a significance analysis.

**Ogive** The graph of a cumulative frequency distribution.

**Omnibus survey** (also known as syndicated survey). Instead of being devoted to one research project, the survey consists of a number of sub-questionnaires, each one being a survey in its own right. This technique is undertaken by market research specialists who offer space on their master questionnaire.

**One-tail test** A significance test in which the null hypothesis can be upset by values well above the mean or by values well below the mean, *but not both*.

**Operating characteristic** The probability of accepting a lot in a sampling inspection procedure (some sources use this term for the probability of rejecting the lot).

**Outcome node** A point on a decision tree leading to a set of possible outcomes.

**Outer control line** One of the two lines on a control chart which serves as an action limit. It is usually set at 3.09 standard errors from the mean.

**Panel data** A survey conducted among a representative sample of individuals. The members of the panel maintain a diary or log of their actions, e.g., which television programs they watched.

**Parameter** A collective name given to statistical measures (usually of the population) such as the arithmetic mean and the standard deviation.

**Percentile** A 100th part of a cumulative frequency.

**Permutation** The number of selections of a given number of objects from a population where order is relevant and the choices are made without replacement.

**Pictogram** A chart in which picture symbols are used to represent values.

**Pie chart** A diagram in which the relative frequencies are represented by sectors of a circle.

**Poisson distribution** A very important discrete probability distribution which has been found to describe such random phenomena as the incidence of accidents and radioactive emissions and disintegrations.

**Positive correlation** Another term used for direct correlation.

**Positive skew** The description of a distribution in which more than half of the area is to the right of the mode.

**Primary data** Original data gathered specifically for the current investigation.

**Process average per cent defective (PAPD)** The percentage of defectives produced by a production process.

**Producer's risk** The probability of a good lot being rejected by the consumer.

**Product moment correlation coefficient** The unabbreviated name for the correlation coefficient.

**Quality control** A method used in industry to ensure the uniformity of a certain product.

**Quartile deviation** Another term for the semi interquartile range.

**Random sampling** A method of selecting a sample in such

a way that every member of the population has an equal and known chance of being selected.

**Range** The difference between the highest and lowest values of a set of observations – a crude measure of dispersion but it does have applications in quality control.

**Rank correlation** The degree of association between two sets of ranks.

**Raw data** Data which are recorded in the way or order in which they are obtained.

**Regression coefficient** The gradient of the line of best fit.

**Regression constant** The intercept on the vertical axis of the line of best fit.

**Regression line** The line of best fit of a pair of variables.

**Rejection region** *see* Critical region.

**Relative frequency** The frequency divided by the total number of observations – sometimes called the statistical probability.

**Residual variation** The sum of squares attributable to random fluctuations.

**Sample frame** The list from which a sample is selected.

**Sampling distribution** The probability distribution of the sample statistic.

**Sampling inspection** A technique used to avoid full screening of a batch of articles. It helps the buyer to estimate the quality of the goods.

**Scatter diagram** A graph depicting paired observations.

**Seasonal variation** The cyclical variation that can be attributed to the time of the year.

**Secondary data** Data already gathered or published by another organization.

**Semi inter-quartile range** A measure of dispersion – half the difference between the two quartiles.

**Sequential analysis** A sampling plan in which the size of the sample is determined by the properties of previous observations.

**Significance test** A statistical decision method such as the *t*-test, the *F*-test and the $\chi^2$ test.

**Skewness** A measure of the "lop-sidedness" of a distribution.

**Standard deviation** The most commonly used method of dispersion – the square root of the mean squared deviations from the mean.

**Standard error** A term for the standard deviation of a sample statistic.

**Standardized normal distribution** A particular normal distribution with a mean of 0 and a standard deviation of 1 (tabulated in Appendix).

**Statistic** Collective name given to statistical measures (usually of the sample) such as the standard deviation or the arithmetic mean.

**Statistical probability** A probability determined from past observations (relative frequency).

**Stratification sampling** A process used to ensure that different strata of the population (such as age) are represented in a sample, in the correct proportion.

**Subjective probability** A probability measuring a person's degree of belief or strength of conviction.

**Sum of squares** Strictly speaking, this means the sum of the squares of a set of observations but, in the analysis of variance, it means the sum of the squares of the **deviations** from the mean.

**System capacity** The maximum number of customers, including those being served, that a queuing system can hold.

**t-distribution** An important continuous probability distribution used for tests of significance on small samples.

**Theoretical probability** A probability assigned by considerations of symmetry.

**Two-tail test** A significance test in which the null hypothesis can be upset by values both well above the mean and well below the mean.

**Type I error** The probability of rejecting the null hypothesis when it is in fact true.

**Type II error** The probability of accepting the null hypothesis when it is in fact false.

**Unimodal** Frequency or probability distribution with one mode.

**Variance** The square of the standard deviation.